TALKING SCHOOLS

By the same author

Anarchy in Action
Streetwork: The Exploding School (with Anthony Fyson)
Vandalism
Tenants Take Over
Housing: An Anarchist Approach
The Child in the City
Art and the Built Environment (with Eileen Adams)
Arcadia for All (with Dennis Hardy)
When We Build Again
Goodnight Campers (with Dennis Hardy)
Chartres: The Making of a Miracle
The Allotment: Its Landscape and Culture (with David Crouch)
The Child in the Country
Undermining the Central Line (with Ruth Rendell)
Welcome, Thinner City: Urban Survival in the 1990s
Images of Childhood (with Tim Ward)
Talking Houses
Freedom To Go: After the Motor Age
Influences: Voices of Creative Dissent
New Town, Home Town

FREEDOM PRESS publish *Freedom* (fortnightly) and *The Raven* (quarterly) as well as books (more than sixty titles in print).

FREEDOM PRESS BOOKSHOP carries the most comprehensive stock of anarchist literature including titles from North America. Please send for our current list.

Freedom Press
in Angel Alley
84b Whitechapel High Street
London E1 7QX

TALKING SCHOOLS

ten lectures by
Colin Ward

FREEDOM PRESS
LONDON
1995

First published
by
FREEDOM PRESS
84b Whitechapel High Street
London E1 7QX
in
1995

ISBN 0 900384 81 6

Typeset by Jayne Clementson
Printed in Great Britain by Aldgate Press, London E1 7RQ

Contents

Foreword

I seem to have been involved with the education industry in various capacities for many decades. For, apart from the 1930s which were my own primary and secondary school years, all through the 1950s I was working on the drawing-board on the design of schools while writing the 'People and Ideas' column for *Freedom*, which often reflected the continuing debate on education. Indeed, I was later to edit a book on the lessons of modern school buildings. In the 1960s I became a teacher, while editing the monthly *Anarchy*, which discussed every conceivable aspect of schools and schooling. In the 1970s as education officer for a poor but lively voluntary body I visited hundreds of schools, while editing *BEE*, the *Bulletin of Environmental Education*, which was addressed to teachers of every subject on the timetable. I wrote several books for reluctant readers and collaborated on two for teachers.

All this made me the kind of person who is asked to talk at teachers' conferences and courses, meetings of educational pressure groups and all those occasions where schooling is on the agenda. As I explained in my book *Talking Houses*, I am not a natural public speaker and always prepared a text, even though I frequently departed from it. It saves a great deal of time spent fumbling for the right word. I frequently provided a sheet of paper with a list of further reading for my listeners.

Needless to say, I often gave substantially the same lecture to different audiences, though attempting to relate the subject to the place we were in and the specific concerns of the people there. I also often recycled the words in various books. Frequently the specialist audience and its response was a testing ground for my approach. Out of the piles of paper on my shelves I have gathered the texts of ten lectures given over a period of twenty years. (For although I announced in 1980 that my platform days were over, half of these were delivered after that date.)

The texts are unchanged except for the first lecture which was a response to the frequent request from student teachers asking what they should read about the anarchists and education. This has been updated several times, as the anarchist literature on education has grown. I have tried to cut out repetitions.

All these lectures were given to audiences of teachers, except for the seventh, which was addressed to architects and administrators, and the ninth, which was given to social workers and people concerned with child welfare and children's play. It may be that I have been lucky in meeting that section of the teaching profession who take the trouble to attend conferences and courses in their particular speciality, but I have developed a profound respect for the people who pursue that demanding occupation five days a week in a political climate in which their work has been denigrated by their political masters whose tenure of office as Secretary of State for Education is considered long if it actually lasts one school year.

In the last lecture in this book I quote the remark of Her Majesty's Chief Inspector of Schools in January 1995 that the real impediment to the development of a better educational system in Britain is "a commitment to particular beliefs about the purposes and conduct of education". I, on the other hand, feel privileged to have met so many teachers who take education seriously.

Colin Ward

1. The Anarchists and Schools

My political attitude is that of anarchism, which is the definition written for the *Encyclopaedia Britannica* by its best-known spokesman, Peter Kropotkin, is "the name given to a principle or theory of life and conduct under which society is conceived without government – harmony in such a society being obtained, not by submission to law, or by obedience to any authority, but by free agreements concluded between the various groups, territorial and professional, freely constituted for the sake of production and consumption, as also for the satisfaction of the infinite variety of needs and aspirations of a civilised being".[1]

Such an ideology is bound to have implications for anarchist attitudes to schools and schooling, and indeed the editors of one of the many recent anthologies of anarchist writings remark that from the school prospectus issued by William Godwin in 1783 to Paul Goodman's book of 1964 *Compulsory Miseducation*, "anarchism has persistently regarded itself as having distinctive and revolutionary implications for education. Indeed, no other movement whatever has assigned to educational principles, concepts, experiments and practices a more significant place in its writings and activities".[2] This remark is amply justified, yet when I was first asked to talk on this topic at the Institute of Education, there was hardly anything in its vast library to which I could refer my listeners for a quick conspectus of anarchist opinions on schools and schooling. But while the educational climate has worsened,

Lecture at the Institute of Education, University of London, May 1975, and last updated in 1994.

the range of accessible literature on anarchist views and experiences has widened, and this is why I'm handing out a booklist of half a dozen recent books in the hope that you will seek them out.

To my mind the most impressive anarchist philosopher of education was the earliest: William Godwin (1756-1836), who is best known as the husband of Mary Wollstonecraft and the father of Mary Shelley. When I trained as a teacher in the 1960s, I resolved to write my dissertation on his educational ideas, and quickly found that the then standard textbooks like *Doctrines of the Great Educators* made no mention of him and that, apart from his *Enquiry Concerning Political Justice*, now a Penguin Classic, it was dauntingly hard to get a sight of facsimiles or photocopies of his specifically educational writings.[3] Happily, his best recent biographer, Peter Marshall, has included a good selection of them in his book of extracts from Godwin.[4] His critics described him as "cold as ice" but his educational proposals reveal him to be as passionately "on the side of the child" as Mary Wollstonecraft, and I have suggested that someone who enjoys that kind of research might analyse the influences on each other of these remarkable propagandists for the freedom of children.[5]

Godwin's first educational tract was published in 1783 as *An account of the seminary that will be opened on Monday the Fourth Day of August, at Epsom in Surrey, for the Instruction of Twelve Pupils*. It failed to convince enough parents and the school never opened. In this pamphlet he declared that "modern education not only corrupts the heart of our youth, by the rigid slavery to which it condemns them, it also undermines their reason, by the unintelligible jargon with which they are overwhelmed in the first instance, and the little attention that is given to accommodating their pursuits to their capacities in the second". And he added that "there is not in the world a truer object of pity than a child terrified at every glance and watching with anxious uncertainty the caprices of a pedagogue".

He did not believe in a solitary education at home, nor did he want large schools. If he had lived 200 years later he would be a supporter of the National Association for the Support of

Small Schools. He wanted the advantages of a social community, not in order to arouse the spirit of competition but because of the importance of *socialisation* in childhood: "I would wish to see the connection of pupils consisting only of pleasure and generosity. They should learn to love and not to hate each other."

Godwin's book *The Enquirer* of 1797 contains, as Peter Marshall rightly says, "some of the most remarkable and advanced ideas on education ever written". Its first words are the splendid affirmation that "the true object of education, like that of every other moral process, is the generation of happiness". And it goes on to assert the rights of the child against the automatic assumptions of authority of the adult world. I could quote his eighteenth-century rhetoric all night, but will content myself with one observation:

Children, it is said, are free from the cares of the world. Are they without their cares? Of all cares, those that bring with them the greatest consolation are the cares of independence. There is no more certain source of exultation than the consciousness that I am of some importance in the world. A child usually feels that he is nobody. Parents, in the abundance of their providence, take good care to administer to them this bitter recollection. How suddenly does a child rise to an enviable degree of happiness, who feels that he has the honour to be trusted and consulted by his superiors?[6]

Between these two resounding manifestos came Godwin's most famous book, his *Enquiry Concerning Political Justice* in 1793. In the course of this book he diverged sharply from progressive opinion in Britain and from the Enlightenment philosophers Rousseau, Helvetius, Diderot and Condorcet, all of whom put forward schemes for national systems of schooling, postulating an ideal state, which in Godwin's view was a contradiction in terms. He had three cogent objections, which I will condense as far as I can:

The injuries that result from a system of national education are, in the first place, that all public establishments include in them the idea of permanence ... public education has always expended its energies in the support of prejudice ... This feature runs through every species of public establishment; and even in the petty institutions of Sunday schools, the chief lessons to be taught are a superstitious veneration for the Church of England, and to bow to every man in handsome coat ...

Secondly, the idea of national education is founded in an inattention to the nature of mind. Whatever each man does for himself is done well; whatever his neighbours or his country undertake to do for him is done ill. It is our wisdom to incite men to act for themselves, not to retain them in a state of perpetual pupillage ... Thirdly, the project of a national education ought uniformly to be discouraged on account of its obvious alliance with national government. This is an alliance of a more formidable nature than the old and much contested alliance of church and state. Before we put so powerful a machine under the direction of so ambitious an agent, it behoves us to consider well what we do. Government will not fail to employ it to strengthen its hand and perpetuate its institutions ... Their views as instigators of a system of education will not fail to be analogous to their views in their political capacity ... (Even) in the countries where liberty chiefly prevails, it is reasonably to be assumed that there are important errors, and a national system has the most direct tendency to perpetuate those errors and to form all minds on one model.[7]

Now I've known admirers of Godwin's thought who are embarrassed by this rejection of 'progressive' opinion and who recollect the hard struggle to achieve free, universal, compulsory education for all under the Education Act of 1870, much delayed by silly disputes between the lobbies of the Church of England and the non-conformist factions, and not actually made effective until years later. A centenary publication from the National Union of Teachers explained that "apart from religious and charitable schools, 'dame' or common schools were operated by the private enterprise of people who were often barely literate", and it explained the widespread working-class hostility to the School Boards with the remark that "parents were not always quick to appreciate the advantages of full-time schooling against the loss of extra wages".[8]

But more recent historians have shown this resistance to state schooling in a quite different light. Stephen Humphries found that working-class private schools (as opposed to what we mean today by private schools) were, by the 1860s, providing an alternative education to that of the charitable, 'National' or 'British' schools, for approximately one-third of all working-class school children, and he suggests that:

This enormous demand for private as opposed to public education is perhaps best illustrated by the fact that working-class parents in a number of major cities responded to the introduction of compulsory attendance regulations not by sending their children to provided state schools, as government inspectors had predicted, but by extending the length of their child's education in private schools. Parents favoured these schools for a number of reasons: they were small and close to home and were consequently more personal and more convenient than most publicly provided schools; they were informal and tolerant of irregular attendance and unpunctuality; no attendance registers were kept; they were not segregated according to age and sex; they used individual as opposed to authoritarian teaching methods; and, most important, they belonged to and were controlled by the local community rather than being imposed on the neighbourhood by an alien authority.[9]

I find this observation very significant and it was reinforced by a mass of contemporary statistical evidence exhumed by Philip Gardner in his book on *The Lost Elementary Schools of Victorian England*.[10] This author concluded that working-class schools, set up by working-class people in working-class neighbourhoods, "achieved just what the customer wanted: quick results in basic skills like reading, writing and arithmetic, wasted no time on religious studies and moral uplift, and represented a genuinely alternative approach to childhood learning to that prescribed by the education experts". In the view of the historian Paul Thompson, the price of eliminating these schools through the imposition of the national education system was "the suppression in countless working-class children of the appetite for education and ability to learn independently which contemporary progressive education seeks to rekindle".[11]

It is certainly ironical that the centenary of state education in Britain was accompanied by a chorus of Marxist sociologists explaining that the function of the public education system has been to Learn to Labour: to slot working-class children into working-class jobs, now that these traditional jobs have disappeared. I am anxious to learn whether the History of Education courses for teachers in training include the recent findings which support Godwin's warnings. But I must turn to later anarchist educational insights.

Historians of anarchist ideas tend, rightly or wrongly, to work their way through a series of Big Thinkers, chronologically through William Godwin, Pierre-Joseph Proudhon, Michael Bakunin and Peter Kropotkin. The more thorough of them also examine the German advocate of 'conscious egoism',

Max Stirner (who was a teacher by profession), the
educational ideas of Leo Tolstoy and his observations of the
school he started at Yasnaya Polyana, and the Spanish teacher
and founder of the 'Modern School' movement, Francisco
Ferrer.[12]

It is certainly remarkable how an anarchist approach led a
variety of anarchist thinkers to offer educational opinions in
anticipation of the progressive opinion of a century later. For
example, Bakunin, in a mere footnote to a polemic about
something else, envisaged the school as a lifelong educational
resource: "They will be schools no longer; they will be popular
academies, in which neither pupils nor masters will be known,
where the people will come freely to get, if they need it, free
instructions, and in which, rich in their own experience, they
will teach in their turn many things to the professors who shall
bring them knowledge which they lack. This then will be a
mutual instruction, an act of intellectual fraternity".[13]

He was writing in 1870 and if this argument about the future
of schooling is familiar to you it is precisely because identical
aspirations were expressed a century later by people like Ivan
Illich and Paul Goodman, or in this country and in this
building by people like Michael Young and Professor Harry
Rée, who told an audience of young teachers that "I think we
are going to see in your lifetime the end of schools as we know
them. Instead there will be a community centre with the doors
open twelve hours a day, seven days a week, where anybody
can wander in and out of the library, workshops, sports centre,
self-service store and bar. In a hundred years time the
compulsory attendance laws for children to go to school may
have gone the same way as the compulsory laws for attendance
at church".[14]

I suspect, however, that for many people the actual practice
of anarchist ideas in education is more interesting than the
theories. For most of us, the most influential and
longest-lasting of 'progressive' schooling in Britain is
Summerhill School, and its founder A.S. Neill. Neill was
suspicious of the embrace of the anarchist movement, though
friendly and welcoming to individual anarchists like me. I
would advise you to read Jonathan Croall's two excellent

books on Neill.[15]

But if you want to read just a couple of general surveys of the anarchist and schools, I have just two to press on you, as both of them are concerned with both theory and experience in and out of the official education system. The first is Michael Smith's *The Libertarians and Education*.[16] When this book appeared I was asked to review it for a teachers' journal. I responded eagerly, anxious to publicise it, but my review was rejected, which left me downcast, not on my account but on Smith's. He reminds us that when A.S. Neill's first book, *A Dominie's Log* was published in 1915, one reviewer was scandalised by the fact that the author seemed totally ignorant of a tradition in progressive education, and offered him, as teacher-trainers are wont to do and just as I am doing today, a reading list. It consisted of names like Rousseau, Pestalozzi, Froebel, Montessori and Dewey.

Michael Smith suggests that a more appropriate reading list for a teacher of Neill's turn of mind would have been Godwin, Proudhon, Tolstoy, Robin and Ferrer. This is interesting, firstly because most teachers would not, then or now, have heard of most of these alternative gurus and those they did know would not be thought about in an educational context, and secondly because Smith is one of the very few to make a distinction between the liberal/progressive educators and the libertarian/anarchist ones.

The handful of people who have sought to put their ideas of 'free' education into practice have always been so beleaguered by the amused hostility of the institutionalised education system on the one hand and by the popular press on the other (with its photographers anxious to get shots of the children smoking, dancing naked in the dew or knocking nails into the grand piano) that they have tended to close ranks and minimise their differences. Neill just couldn't stand the high-minded and manipulative progressives. By the 1930s he was writing to Dora Russell of Beacon Hill School that she and he were "the only educators". As one of his mentors, Homer Lane, put it: "'Give the child freedom' is the insistent cry of the New Educators, but then its exponents usually devise a 'system' which, although based on the soundest of

principles, limits that freedom and contradicts the principle."
Lane was echoing the opinion of William Godwin in *The
Enquirer*, where he found that Rousseau, even though the
world was indebted to him "for the irresistible energy of his
writings, and the magnitude of his speculations" had fallen
into the common error of manipulating the child. "His whole
system of education is a series of tricks, a puppet-show
exhibition, of which the master holds the wires, and the
scholar is never to suspect in what manner they are moved".
Dr Smith's survey of anarchist approaches to education
distinguishes between the libertarian *position* and the
libertarian *movement*. He shares my enthusiasm for Godwin
and before moving on to the concept of Integral Education
developed by the French anarchists, he visits Harmony, the
utopian community envisaged by Charles Fourier, whose
educational ideals were directed, naturally, towards social
harmony and the minimisation of the exercise of authority.
What endears Fourier to me is his proposal that in the primary
years education should be arranged around cooking and
opera, these being activities which developed all the human
arts and skills and which did not rely on booklearning. They
would also be fun. In the secondary years the unruly impulses
of children were to be channelled into socially valuable work.
"Fourier envisaged two main independent child societies: the
Little Hordes and the Little Bands. The Little Hordes would
reflect children's taste for dirt and excitement. They would
keep Harmony clean, repair roads, kill poisonous snakes, feed
the animals and so on. Their highly necessary tasks were
menial in themselves, but precisely because they were seen as
nasty by the adult world and because they were performed for
the community, the Little Hordes would be highly honoured.
They would have special dress and badges of distinction, they
would ride horses and would go about their work to the
accompaniment of music ... The Little Bands would be more
concerned with cultural matters, they would cultivate dress
and good manners, would care for the sick and would tend
the plants and vegetables."
As Michael Smith comments, though it all sounds nutty, the
psychology is not at all askew. The child is given a valued social

role. He then moves on to Bakunin and Proudhon. Proudhon was the craftsman son of a peasant, and both his political and educational thinking reflected this:

Proudhon was always conscious of the fact that the children he was talking about were the children of workers. Work was going to be their life when they grew up. Proudhon saw nothing wrong with this. The work a man did was something to be proud of, it was what gave interest, value and dignity to his life. It was right, therefore, that school should prepare the young for a life of work. That is: an education that was entirely bookish or grammar-schoolish in conception, was valueless from the point of view of ordinary working-class children. Of course, an education that went too far in the other direction, which brought up children merely to be fodder for factories, was equally unacceptable. What was required was an education which would equip a child for the workplace but would also give him a degree of independence in the labour market. This could be achieved by giving him not just the basis of a trade but, as well, a whole range of marketable skills which would ensure that he was not totally at the mercy of an industrial system which required specialisation of its workers and then discarded them when the specialisation was no longer of interest to the firm. Thus Proudhon was led to the idea of an education that was 'polytechnical'.

You will have guessed, correctly, that Proudhon was concerning himself solely with the education of boys, but this was not true of his successors like Kropotkin with his opinions on the integration of brain work and manual work, nor of others like Ferrer whose approach was similarly that of education for *emancipation* as opposed to education to meet the needs of industry or the state, which they saw as education for *subservience*. This leads Smith to some of his most interesting pages for the English-speaking reader, when he describes 'Integral Education' in practice through the experience of the French anarchist Paul Robin and the school he ran from 1880 to 1894 at Cempius. It was based on workshop training and the abandonment of the classroom in favour of what we would now call the resource centre. Cooking, sewing, carpentry and metalwork were undertaken by both sexes, and "the Cempius children, both girls and boys, were among the first children in France to go in for cycling". Co-education, sexual equality and atheism brought Robin's downfall, but another celebrated French anarchist, Sebastien Faure, ran a school called La Ruche (The Beehive). "Faure had learned one very significant lesson from Robin's downfall:

to stay completely out of the state system and so be assured
of complete independence". Smith takes us through the
experience of Tolstoy and Ferrer and concludes by relating
the varied traditions of libertarian pedagogy from the past, to
the widely-read authors of the 1960s and 1970s who we lump
together as the 'de-schoolers', all of them published in
widely-circulated cheap editions by Penguin Education in
those days, John Holt, Paul Goodman, George Dennison,
Paulo Freire and Ivan Illich.

Finally I turn to a changing group of people who, as the
Libertarian Education Collective, have published the journal
Lib ED as "a magazine for the liberation of learning" since
1966. Files of this journal will be found in the libraries of
virtually all teacher-training institutions and an index to its
contents as well as general bibliographies and addresses are to
be found in their publication *Freedom in Education*.[17] One of
their number, John Shotton, has produced a large-scale survey
of a century of educational experiment in Britain.[18] In my
foreword to this book I explained that one reason for its
importance was that it was in effect the final part of a trilogy
of recent books by authors in different fields which, "through
painstaking and impeccable research, have turned the
standard histories of education and their assumptions upside
down". The first two were the books I have mentioned by
Stephen Humphries and Philip Gardner. For the opening
section of Shotton's book rescues from "the enormous
condescension of posterity" in the now-famous phrase of E.P.
Thompson's a whole series of local working-class libertarian
schools and Sunday schools in Britain in the early years of this
century. He calls this section "The Thirst for Knowledge" –
a reminder to us in the profoundly anti-educational climate
of contemporary schooling that there were, and are, times and
places when schooling was and is valued for its own sake.

He goes on to describe a century of private ventures in
libertarian education, with the usual names of Summerhill,
Dartington Hall, Burgess Hill, Kilquhanity and Beacon Hill,
and some lesser-known private adventures. This is followed
by his description of a similar variety of libertarian schools for
the unschoolable, and an account of efforts to introduce

libertarian education into state schooling, with a description of Prestolee in Lancashire (Teddy O'Neill), St George-in-the-East in Stepney (Alex Bloom), Braehead School and Summerhill Academy in Scotland (R.F. Mackenzie) and Countesthorpe College in Leicestershire where Shotton himself was a teacher. Finally he tells the story of over a dozen examples of the 'deschooling' movement in British cities between 1960 and 1990. Shotton makes no claims that cannot be backed up by evidence and he looks specifically for the evidence provided by children rather than by propagandists.

In the bleak climate of educational reaction in the 1990s, he draws us into unexplored territory and reminds us that experiment is the oxygen of education. It dies without it. This is why the anarchist literature on schools is important for all of us.

Notes

1. Peter Kropotkin, *Anarchism* and *Anarchist Communism*, edited by Nicolas Walter (London, Freedom Press, 1987).

2. Leonard Krimerman and Lewis Parry, *Patterns of Anarchy* (New York, Doubleday Anchor, 1966).

3. Colin Ward, *The Educational Thought of William Godwin* (unpublished special study, Garnett College, London SW15, 1965).

4. Peter Marshall, *William Godwin* (London, Yale University Press, 1984), *The Anarchist Writings of William Godwin* (London, Freedom Press, 1986).

5. Colin Ward, *Influences: Voices of Creative Dissent* (Devon, Green Books, 1991).

6. William Godwin, *The Enquirer: Reflections on Education, Manners and Literature* (London, G.G. and J. Robinson, 1797; facsimile reprint New York, Augustus J. Kelley, 1965). His school prospectus is reprinted in William Godwin, *Four Early Pamphlets*, edited by B.R. Pollin (Gainsville, Florida, 1965).

7. William Godwin, *Enquiry Concerning Political Justice* (London, G.G. and J. Robinson, 1793; reprint of third edition edited by Isaac Kramnick, Harmondsworth, Penguin Classics, 1976). I should mention that the task of scholars has been eased by the availability in university libraries of Marilyn Butler and Janet Todd (editors) *The Complete Works of Mary Wollstonecraft* (six volumes, Pickering, 1989), Mark Philp *et al* (editors) *The Collected Novels and Memoirs of William Godwin* (eight volumes, Pickering & Chatto, 1992) and Mark Philp *et al* (editors) *The Political and Philosophical Writings of William Godwin* (seven volumes, Pickering & Chatto, 1994).

8. National Union of Teachers, *The Struggle for Education* (London, NUT, 1970).

9. Stephen Humphries, *Hooligans or Rebels? An Oral History of Working-Class Childhood and Youth 1889-1939* (Oxford, Basil Blackwell, 1981).

10. Philip Gardner, *The Lost Elementary Schools of Victorian England* (London, Croom Helm, 1984).

11. Paul Thompson, 'Basic Skills' in *New Society*, 6th December 1984.

12. For general histories of anarchism see George Woodcock, *Anarchism: A History of Libertarian Ideas and Movements* (Harmondsworth, Penguin, 1963) and Peter Marshall, *Demanding the Impossible: A History of Anarchism* (London, HarperCollins, 1992). For the American impact of Francisco Ferrer see Paul Avrich, *The Modern School Movement: Anarchism and Education in the United States* (New Jersey, Princeton University Press, 1980).

13. Michael Bakunin, *God and the State* (London, Freedom Press, 1910; New York, Dover Publications, 1970).

14. Reported in *The Teacher*, 8th April 1972.

15. Jonathan Croall, *Neill of Summerhill: The Permanent Rebel* (London, Routledge & Kegan Paul, 1983); Jonathan Croall (editor) *All the Best, Neill: Letters from Summerhill* (London, Andre Deutsch, 1974).

16. Michael P. Smith, *The Libertarians and Education* (London, Allen & Unwin, 1983).

17. *Freedom in Education: a do-it-yourself guide to the liberation of learning* (Libertarian Education, Phoenix House, 170 Wells Road, Bristol BS4 2AG, 1992).

18. John Shotton, *No Master High or Low: Libertarian Education and Schooling 1890-1990* (Bristol, Libertarian Education, 1993).

2. Education for Mastery of the Environment

In the schools of most European countries there has been a great deal of attention to environmental education during the last five years. Several international organisations have held conferences on this theme and issued manifestos, though it is hard to say what effect this has had in ordinary secondary school classrooms. The phrase itself is deeply equivocal. It can imply, for example, the *use* of the environment – instead of the classroom – as an educative medium (a point of view which reaches its logical conclusion in the ideas of the 'de-schoolers' like Paul Goodman or Ivan Illich), or it can simply imply education *about* the environment, treated as a classroom subject like mathematics or French.

The interpretation of its subject matter is also equivocal. Architects and planners often assume that more and better environmental education in schools will help to close the gap between their own activities and popular sentiments. But in fact, for most people, including most teachers, 'environmental education' is interpreted as education about the *natural* environment, which is 'good' and the threat to it from the *built* environment which is 'bad' (on the unspoken assumption that God made the countryside and Man made the town). Or it is considered to be education about the conservation of natural resources, the crisis of energy and consumption, or about

Lecture at the UNESCO/UNEP course on Urban Education, London, March 1977, published in translation in this form in *Spazio e Società* (Milan) No 4, December 1978.

pollution and its effect on the habitat.

Much less often is 'environmental education' considered to be concerned with the towns and cities where most of the children of Europe live and where most of them go to school. As recently as 1975, English teachers addressing conferences on the subject organised by UNESCO or by the Council of Europe found that their colleagues in other countries were surprised that the built environment should be considered a major theme of environmental education. This is not to suggest that British schools as a whole are more advanced in this area than those of any other country. Very often it is the enthusiasm, the tenacity and the understanding of an individual teacher that is important, rather than any provision in the official curriculum of the school. Very often too the teacher is frustrated by the examination system, the syllabus of school subjects, the timetable or the whole organisation of the school. Very often the impetus for education about the built environment comes from *outside* the school.

The situation in Britain

In the late 1960s dissatisfaction with the results of planning policies in Britain led to the slogan of 'public participation in planning', just as in the United States it led to ideas about 'advocacy planning'. The government appointed a committee led by Arthur Skeffington which produced a report *People and Planning* (London, HMSO, 1969), which among other things recommended that education about town planning should be "part of the way in which all secondary schools make children conscious of their future civic duties" and that it should be "part of the liberal and civic studies within places of further education", and that the training of teachers should include "a similar emphasis on civic studies, including the philosophy of town and country planning".

The Department of Education and Science totally ignored these recommendations (in Britain the actual curriculum of schools is not officially the concern of central government, but of local education authorities and of the Schools Council, a body financed jointly by local and central government) but they were not ignored by the Town and Country Planning

Association, a voluntary organisation founded in 1899 by Ebenezer Howard, which in 1971 set up its Education Unit to advise teachers. Five years of work in this field have confirmed our original conviction that our task was *not* to encourage teachers to give lectures on the principles of town and country planning, or the legislative basis governing their application, but to encourage education for mastery of the environment, aiming at a situation where the skills to manipulate the environment are accessible to all the people, not merely to an articulate minority. If the aim of environmental education is not to make children the masters of their environment, what else can it be for?

But how can we devise an approach to environmental education which really engages the ordinary child in school? Many educators advocate a study of the locality as the starting point. But in the very first issue of *BEE* Michael Storm, a well-known English lecturer in education, remarked that there was no other area of the school curriculum with such a gap between universally accepted policy and actual practice, and no area which so readily produced an inevitable disillusionment for the teacher. He continued:

Despite a considerable experience of orthodox 'local study' in history, geography and social studies, pupils are ill-equipped to understand the *processes* at work in their society affecting the environment. The treatment of local themes in such a way as to interest young people requires much thought, much preparation – and a degree of sophistication which is often lacking. Quantities of information, whether presented didactically or 'discovered' by field observation or from local documentary sources, are not sufficient to guarantee effective 'involvement'. Too often, it appears, programmes of local study set out to deal with the question: 'what should people know about their locality?' An apparently minor alteration of this question to: '*what issues are currently alive in this area?*' would in fact occasion a complete reconsideration of the programme. In the first place, this question implies that there could be no standard approach or content to local studies, since themes will vary according to locality. Yet wherever the school is situated, a problem-oriented approach to local study is possible.

Environmental education is political education

Everything that we have learned about successful environmental education suggests that Michael Storm was right, and this is why we advocate an 'issue-based' approach to the environment. It is this that puts us in the same camp as the Politics Association, another voluntary organisation that seeks a more sophisticated approach to teaching about politics in British schools. Its inspirer, Professor Bernard Crick of London University, declares that "civic education must be aimed at creating citizens. If we want a passive population, leave well alone". He is arguing for the need, in school, to accept conflict over political issues and to avoid presenting *the* system and *the* consensus as some kind of universal truth. "If politics is the recognition and tolerance of diversity, so must be a political or civic education ... To stress deliberately 'what we have in common' and to underplay the differences is both a false account of politics and a cripplingly dull basis for a political education. 'Consensus' is not something to be invoked like spiritual cement to stick together something that would otherwise be broken apart; it is, on the contrary, a quality which arises to ease the continued co-existence of those who have been living together. It is not prior to the experience of a political community; it is a product of that experience, and therefore cannot be meaningfully taught until a person understands, however generally and simply, the actual political problems and controversies of his community."

It was an unwillingness to examine the *politics* of planning which vitiated the educational aspects of European Architectural Heritage Year in many countries. There was more willingness to rhapsodise about our ancient buildings than to examine whose interests were served by destroying them. The Council of Europe said that it was "determined to halt the steady loss of irreplaceable monuments and the erosion of character in historic European towns". This loss and this erosion have not happened because of our neglect of the aesthetic education of the young, but for other reasons. The first is the priority given to the motor vehicle in our cities: the assumption that, at whatever cost, the traffic must get through. The second is speculation in land and property. At the symposium in Rome on the theme 'Common Market: Common Responsibility' in 1964, Malcolm MacEwen said "The soaring cost of land, and the vast profits of the landowners and developers, has led to the rape of cities, and are a poison seeping through the entire fabric of society". The third is the fact that local authorities have often shown themselves to be just as indifferent to our building inheritance as speculators.

An environmental education which ignores these political factors is an education in hypocrisy.

Contact with the thing itself

There has grown up, largely through the activities of the National Parks Service in the USA, a philosophy of environmental interpretation which defines *interpretation* as "an educational activity which aims to reveal meanings and relationships through the use of original objects, by first-hand experience, and by illustrative media, rather than simply to communicate factual information". This implies that in the interpretation of the environment, through contact with *the thing itself* and not with a two-dimensional version of it in the classroom, the child's investigation of the urban environment must be made in the town itself, through what geographers call *fieldwork*, or what in an urban context we may call *streetwork*.

Everyone will agree that generations of urban children received an environmental education in the street. Bernard Rudofsky notes that there was a time when to a child the street was "an open book, superbly illustrated, thoroughly familiar, yet inexhaustible". But most city children today live in what we might call an attenuated environment, an urban context in which the traditional attributes of the street culture are missing. The rebuilt modern city has, as Jane Jacobs complained, "abandoned the basic function of the city street, and with it, necessarily, the freedom of the city". For, she says, "under the seeming disorder of the old city, wherever the old city is working successfully, is a marvellous order for maintaining the safety of the streets and the freedom of the city".

You can see the processes she described in her book *The Death and Life of Great American Cities*, at work in any city district which has been fortunate enough to have escaped the attentions of the highways engineer and the property developer, or the sinister combination of the two, and where the street still operates as a street.

But these essential attributes of the street are not taught to architects and planners, let alone to the citizens. They are not cherished by the city fathers, let alone by its children. Our society's efforts, so far as *they* are concerned, are largely devoted to keeping them *off* the streets. can we conceive of a conscious effort at educating a new generation in the functioning of the city, by way of the street?

The vision of Paul Goodman

The ideology of streetwork, the use of the urban environment as *the* educational resource, was enunciated over thirty years ago by the American anarchist Paul Goodman (later the author, with his brother the architect Percival Goodman, of *Communitas*). In his novel *The Grand Piano*, written in 1942, there is a dialogue between a professor and a street urchin:

'On the one hand, this City is the only one you will ever have, and you must make the best of it. On the other hand, if you *want* to make the best of it, you've got to be able to criticise it and change it and circumvent it ... It seems to me *prima facie* that we have to use the City itself as our school. Instead of bringing imitation bits of the City into a school building, let us go at our own pace and get out among the real things. What I envisage is gangs of about six kids, starting at nine or ten years old, roving the City with a shepherd empowered to protect them, and accumulating experiences tempered to their powers.'

'Holy cats!' cried Horace, wide-eyed at the thought of others behaving as he did. 'They'd surely make trouble and stop the traffic!'

'So much the worse for the traffic', said the professor flatly. 'I am talking about the primary function of social life, to educate a better generation, and people tell me that the tradesmen must not be inconvenienced. I proceed. Fundamentally our kids must learn two things: Skills and Sabotage. Let me explain.

'We have here a great City and a vast culture. It must be maintained as a whole; it can and must be improved piecemeal. It is relatively permanent. At the same time it is a vast corporate organisation; its enterprise is bureaucratised, its arts are institutionalised, its *mores* are far from spontaneity: therefore, in order to avoid being swallowed up by it, or stamped on by it, in order to acquire and preserve a habit of freedom, a kid must learn to circumvent it and sabotage it at any needful point as occasion arises.'

'Stop! Stop' said Horace. 'Isn't this a contradiction? You say that we have to learn to be at home in the City, then you say we have to sabotage it. On the one hand we have to love and serve it; on the other hand we have to kick it. Does it make sense to you?'

'There is nothing in what you say, young man. In this City these two attitudes come to the same thing; if you persist in honest service, you will soon be engaging in sabotage. Do you follow that?'

All the characteristics of the ideal pattern of streetwork emerge from this dialogue, as well as the dilemmas of putting it into practice: the questions of the dangers of the street, the size of the group, the role of the shepherd or teacher, and the fact that if we teach the skills to manipulate the environment we are also teaching the skills to sabotage the activities of its destroyers. Much more recently Goodman wrote that the model for the kind of incidental education that he recommended was that of the Athenian pedagogue touring the city with his charges, "but for this the streets and working places of the city must be made safer and more available. The idea of city planning is for the children to be able to use the city, for no city is governable if it does not grow citizens who feel it is theirs".

Climbing the rungs of Arnstein's ladder

An American planner, Sherry Arnstein, devised a 'ladder of participation' as a means of evaluating the genuineness or spuriousness of schemes for community participation in planning. The rungs of her ladder are:

CITIZEN CONTROL

DELEGATED POWER

PARTNERSHIP

PLACATION

CONSULTATION

INFORMING

THERAPY

MANIPULATION

Arnstein's ladder is a very useful device for realistically assessing our ideas about public participation in planning. She uses it to assess American ideas about 'advocacy planning'. In Britain, the Skeffington Report and the current planning legislation are only up to the third or fourth rung of the ladder. If we are to educate for 'citizen control' we have to develop the idea that the school must be allowed to become the *Enquiring* School: a privileged institution, licensed to probe and criticise in the name of the next generation.

Individual teachers in many countries are developing a pattern of environmental education which unconsciously echoes Goodman's approach. The experience and aspirations of many British teachers, for example, were reflected in a film written and directed by Vittorio De Seta for RAI, which was shown on BBC television (I understand that it was an adaptation of a book *Un Anno a Pietralata* by Alberto Bernardini). In this *Diary of a Schoolteacher*, the teacher found that his pupils in a working-class suburb "did not feel that they belonged to the big city" and when they explored the fashionable and ancient city centre they were like "tourists in their own city". A teacher in a poor district of New York or London would find the same.

The teacher's approach to history was to get pupils to investigate the history of their own families, to gather the personal reminiscences of one day in the Second World War from their parents and grandparents. His approach to social studies was to inspire his class to explore the housing of the locality and to produce on the duplicator a "report on the district and its housing problems" and to explore their own future prospects by a study of juvenile employment there.

His activities were not approved by the principal of the school, and in vain he quoted the platitudes of a Ministerial Circular about the "continual awareness of the external environment from which all learning springs".

We all agree with these words, but the teacher who wants to develop this environmental awareness has several obstacles to overcome, quite apart from the ones faced by the teacher in the film. In British schools environmental education is much more developed in the primary school (ages 5 to 11) than in secondary education with its academic constraints: the timetable, examination syllabuses and the artificial limitations of subjects. As a strategy some teachers believe in the institution of a new subject: Environmental Studies. Others think it more useful to work within the framework of existing subjects: geography, history, language, etc. Another difficulty is that many teachers only feel qualified to teach what they have been taught to teach, and nobody taught *them* about urbanism, town planning, architecture and the built environment. They have a superstitious belief that these are professional mysteries into which they have not been initiated. Again the approach through current issues, rather than the accumulation of facts and theories, would help them initiate a genuine educative experience.

Helping the teacher

One of the ways of helping the teacher make a success of education for environmental participation is the dissemination of suitable techniques. Some of these are commonplaces of educational technology, for example getting students to prepare their own slide-tape presentations of the locality, or the use by children of cassette-tape-recorders to interview old inhabitants so as to accumulate the *autobiography of a place*. Others are techniques with particular value in this area of education. The first of these is the use of gaming and simulation. Most teachers who have experimented with simulation and role-playing techniques enthuse about the involvement that they bring to their classes, including that of 'non-academic' children. Gaming techniques readily demonstrate how a conflict of attitudes and values may have a profound effect both on the environmental outcome and on individual perceptions of the environment.

The second new educational resource is the Urban Studies Centre. One development in English education since the war has been the development of Field Centres – residential centres in rural places used by urban schools – which have profoundly affected the way in which subjects like geography and biology are taught, by giving much greater emphasis to first-hand investigation or fieldwork. Several years ago we set up an organisation, CUSC (the Council for Urban Study Centres), to press for urban equivalents to these rural centres. This met with an enthusiastic response and several such centres now exist. An Urban Studies Centre would serve as a base for streetwork by both local and visiting schools. It would have facilities for imaginative audio-visual interpretation of the city's physical structure in its historical, social and economic context. It would be a repository for maps, plans and documents about the place, and would be staffed by a tutor-warden familiar both with the neighbourhood and with the techniques of urban study. If it had residential accommodation, children from other towns or other countries could make a real study of another kind of environment instead of just going round the tourist attractions. The same premises could be used for a Visitor Centre and for a Community Forum – neutral premises for the discussion of local issues between the planners and the planned. The Notting Dale Urban Studies Centre, in a poor district of London, has reprographic facilities which it puts at the disposal of local community groups and tenants' associations.

The third educational resource or technique is the *Town Trail*, again a development from rural education and from the Nature Trails which have been devised to enable people to get as much as possible from a rural walk. The town trail is a guided itinerary depicted on a clear map that the individual child (or adult) can follow alone or in a group. The route will include focus points of special interest, and it is useful for it to have at least one high 'outlook point' on top of a hill or an accessible high building. Trail-making is essentially a local activity: it depends on intimate knowledge of the terrain and is therefore an ideal focus for, and product of, local study. A class should not merely follow a ready-made trail: it should construct its own, in order to get the educational bonus of its own research and presentation. There are too many variations on the Town Trail theme. Apart from visual, architectural or sensory trails, there can be historical, literary or industrial trails, skyline trails, nocturnal trails of horror – designed to highlight what is wrong with a particular part of the environment.

The involvement of architects

Architects are sometimes invited into a school to talk about architecture, but often the school does not make the best use of such wisdom as he can offer. Often the most useful thing an architect can do with a group of children is to take them for a walk down the street. The habit of informed observation is the most precious bit of expertise that he can offer, and that teachers and pupils can absorb from him.

Stanley King is an English architect working in Canada who got involved in a school programme intended to stimulate an interest in the urban environment. He was dismayed by the reactions in the classes he visited. "The atmosphere was anxious, hostile, full of gloom". In short, the students weren't talking. And inevitably, they weren't listening either. When they did talk and listen, he discerned in them a combination of apathy and fear. Apathy because his students had concluded that the city was "too big to fight" and fear because they felt the city to be "like an evil presence creeping up on its people". Many teachers will recognise the defensively cynical stance.

The experience worried Mr King and led him to think about the alienation of the young from the city and of the need to reconcile the generations in a common experiment in environmental participation. His particular approach was determined by his architectural background and his aptitude for rapid sketching. Eventually he abandoned his practice of architecture and set up a 'participation centre' at the University of British Columbia to train teachers in the methods he had developed. He calls the method he evolved the 'design-in' and sees it as the first stage of a four-part process:

1. The design-in, which collects from the people who will use the development *their* ideas and experiences and preferred qualities of life and environment.
2. The sketch designs, made in the architect's office, to include these ideas and arrange them with alternative priorities and with costs.
3. The presentation of the alternative possibilities to the people who vote on the sketch designs to indicate their choice of priorities.
4. The directive by the elected representatives to the architect for final design.

Stanley King quotes a remark by the historian G.M. Trevelyan, that "ugliness remains a quality of the modern city, rendered acceptable by custom to a public that can only imagine what it has seen". The essence of the procedure he has been using is that it not only awakens the participants to alternative possibilities, but enables them to communicate these alternatives. To remain inarticulate, he says, "ensures a continuation of the present scene. The designing of any development intended for public use will eventually comply with the developer's estimate of public opinion. Architects at the design-in stage can offer visions of the future that the developer-client could never permit to appear. I hope that this will build up a reversal of the present city trends."

We may feel sceptical about this hope, but let us watch a design-in. At Port Hawkesbury in Nova Scotia, Stanley King was invited to conduct a design-in with a large group of local people in connection with the planning of a community school (a community centre containing school facilities). This is how he describes the session:

Fifty children sit before the adults of the community, facing a drawing board ten metres long. I invite the children to be the architects and to design a city called 'Some City', and help us to see what might later surround the community school. They are asked first to look at the past to see what made the city into its present shape, and what might shape its future. A small trading community drawn on a shoreline grows larger to include stores and houses. The children suggest solutions to the problems that arise in the community and draw a prosperous town that includes all that comes to mind as belonging to towns and cities. Soon the board is crammed with the buildings and structures of a monstrous modern city. The children dislike the city they have drawn. 'No! I wouldn't want to live there. It's a mess.' They argue over the remedies for the design of the future.

Then he outlines the stages of the design process and invites the participation of the adults and children in indicating what they expect to find in the new community school. The suggestions are written as headings along drawing boards on either side of the hall:

I write a series of questions around a figure called PEP (Personal Experience and Perception) and explain that the answers will guide the designers. The people answer from their own personal experiences and perception and in doing so observe three rules: 1. Avoid criticism of other people's ideas. Ideas must flow in. 2. Make no decision about fitting the ideas together in a structure. 3. Do not try to speak for others. Speak only for oneself.

The teenagers come forward to act as architects. Groups of people form at each named activity. The teenagers question them and note their replies on the drawing board. Soon all the people are engrossed in discussion and the boards are covered with notes and sketches. The adults show surprise at the mature expressions of the young and they in turn show surprise at the perception of the adults. Each listens to the other with respect. Politics and rhetoric are avoided by the rule that each must speak only for himself; argument is avoided by the rule that no decisions are to be attempted at this stage. The absence of criticism fosters an atmosphere of creativity and an air of unity pervades. The design-in, recorded on video-tape, will be played back at a future meeting to collect second thoughts. Already there is ample information for the architects to commence the alternative sketch designs.

The description has a beautiful appropriateness about it: a community, young and old together, preparing the architect's brief for a community facility.

How do children perceive the city?

Such experimental insights as we have about the child's perception of the built environment come – as so often happens in creative research – from the mutual accommodation of ideas from quite separate theoretical approaches. The academic industry of perception studies which is bound to affect the way we approach environmental education brings together the *cognitive mappers* exemplified by Kevin Lynch, and the *developmentalists* exemplified by Jean Piaget. It was Lynch who, in his book *The Image of the City*, introduced us to the notion that people structure their concept of the city around certain elements: (1) *nodes* (the places where human activities meet), (2) *paths*, (3) *edges*, (4) *districts*, and (5) *landmarks*. It was Piaget who, in *The Child's Conception of Space*, set out the developmental theory of perception with its three stages: the pre-operational stage (ages 3 to 9), the concrete operational stage (ages 9 to 13) and finally the formal operational stage.

The young investigators of environmental perception are iconoclastic about the old masters who laid the foundations of their work. They point out that the original American research into the nature of the cognitive maps of our environment which we all carry around in our heads was done with populations who were adult, middle-class, articulate and car-driving. They point out that Piaget's studies of perception in children were done indoors, in a classroom situation, without the stimulus or imaginative interest of work in the environment itself. They indicate too that assumptions about the "level of abstraction" children can cope with at different ages ignore the potentialities of imaginative teaching designed to make these abstractions comprehensible. Educational orthodoxy used to hold, for example, that there was some age before which it was pointless to teach the use of maps because children would not have made the leap from visual to symbolic representation of the environment. Roger Hart told me of the work he did in this field with children aged 7 and 8 in Worcester, Massachusetts. Using low altitude vertical aerial photographs on A4-sized sheets (Ozalid prints which could be made for a few cents each), Hart and the class built up the map of the city on the classroom floor. He asked the children to bring in their matchbox-toy model cars which are made at an appropriate scale for the maps. Then everyone set out on the map to find the way to the city centre. This led them to difficulties of traffic congestion and of finding a place to park. It also resulted in crashes and in the need to get an ambulance through the traffic and back to St Vincent's Hospital.

In an equally simple and pleasurable piece of work in a British context, Brian Goodey of Birmingham graphically established the fundamental truth that people's cognitive maps of the city differ according to their age, social status and lifestyle. You might regard this as so obvious as to need no proving, but if you look at the redevelopment of the central area of any British city you can see that the unspoken assumption has been that the city exists for the adult male middle-class commuter. With the cooperation of a local newspaper, Goodey inserted in the paper a map of central Birmingham with the middle portion omitted so that respondents, who were assessed by age, sex, occupation and mode of travel, could insert their mental maps of the missing portion. The results underlined the observation of Alexander Mitscherlich that "the commercially-oriented planning of our cities is clearly aimed at one age group only – working adults – and even then inadequately enough. How a child is to become a working adult seems to be a negligible factor. The world of the child is a sphere of the socially weak, and is ruthlessly manipulated."

Manipulated or not, it is certain that the child's comprehension of the city differs from that of the adult. Working with architectural students, Jeff Bishop analysed both for content and mapping style, the cognitive maps made by 180 children between the ages of 9 and 16 in the English East Coast port of Harwich. Their findings confirmed those of investigators in American cities. They found significant differences between the maps of boys and girls. Girls included more natural objects. Boys were more advanced into Piaget's third (Euclidean or formal operative) stage than girls of the same age. Walkers, needless to say, provided more detail than bus riders. But the most interesting thing of all was the comparison of the children's maps and those by adults. In the middle of Harwich there is a lighthouse which featured as a significant landmark in the maps drawn by the adults, but none of the Harwich children showed the lighthouse on their maps, though many showed the public lavatory which stands at its base. Things which were important to the children included kiosks, hoardings and other bits of unconsidered clutter in the street. One thing that frequently recurred in their maps (and was totally unnoticed by the adults) was a telephone junction box – a large metal object on the footpath. From a child's point of view it was important, because it could be hidden behind or climbed on. Bishop remarks that if Piaget were to be understood literally, an eight-year-old could not find his way home from school. But how often, he asks, do we give the child the opportunity to show us what he knows about the space in which he moves around? How often do we let the child lead *us* home from school instead of us leading the child?

Teaching about environmental design

I am sure that in most secondary schools nothing is taught about the design of the environment. I think it likely that very often when something is taught it is about the history of architecture, or about 'good taste', and that it is *not* education for mastery of the environment. The whole matter of teaching about design in the environment is rather like nibbling at the petals of an artichoke. The rather coarse outer layer, now looking very over-ripe, consists of that view of the urban scene as a series of gems or jewels, usually hallowed by association with religion or with the aristocracy: all those cathedrals and palaces.

Beyond this layer is that which seeks to inculcate the structural or stylistic significance of the building, and its place in the historical development of architecture. For most children this approach is stultifyingly boring, and it is also totally one-sided since it concentrates its attention on 'official' architecture rather than on the heritage of vernacular buildings. After this comes a layer which recognises the irrelevancy of historicism and seeks to take the pupils through the landmarks of contemporary architecture (usually preaching the orthodoxies of twenty years ago), but at least asking them to evaluate the contemporary additions to the urban scene.

We have now reached the part of the artichoke where the petals are most succulent, where there is less and less unassimilable material to be left at the side of the plate. Here we have a teacher who realises that the *whole* of the built environment is worthy of examination through direct experience, through contact with *the thing itself*. This teacher is concerned that the pupils should examine houses and housing (and every city is a museum of different ideas about housing design), and should look at the architecture of industry and transport. Not only this, but he devises techniques which enable his class to look beyond the character of individual buildings and to evaluate the whole townscape, the spaces enclosed by buildings, the function of their height in relation to the width of the street, the effect of changes of level, the role of decoration on surfaces, the play of light and shadows. We want them to ask, as an English art educator Ralph Jeffery asks, "What is good and bad about this habitat? What is superfluous? What could be done to improve it? Is it harsh, soft, hostile, friendly, man-scaled, dramatic, relevant to modern lifestyles? Does anyone love it, would anyone miss is, does it generate *topophilia*?"

By now we are at the heart of the artichoke: the best part of all. Perhaps this takes the form of getting the school to design and build some extension to the school building itself. Of course this cannot happen every year, and is always faced with an incredible amount of official obstruction. Behind such an activity is the hallowed assumption that we learn by doing. But behind it too is the knowledge that by demystifying the manipulation of the environment we are changing the politics of environmental decision-making. The grandiose claims of the environmental professions for their specialised and exclusive wisdom – whether we are talking about architects, planners or highway engineers – have been exploded, not by alternative ideologies but simply because the results of their activities are there for all to see.

Towards a malleable environment

We are groping for a different political theory and for a different aesthetic theory. The missing political element is the politics of participation. The missing cultural element is the aesthetic of a variable, manipulable, malleable environment, an environment of 'loose parts'. Simon Nicholson (of the British Open University) who evolved the theory of loose parts, sets it out thus:

In any environment, both the degree of inventiveness and creativity and the possibility of discovery, are directly proportional to the number and kind of variables in it.

I cannot do better than to quote the argument he uses to explain the way in which he arrives at this principle in order to illustrate why education, in the school and out of it, has such an important part to play. Nicholson claims that the imposed environment, the one in which the citizen has a merely passive part to play, results from cultural élitism. He says:

Creativity is for the gifted few: the rest of us are compelled to live in environments constructed by the gifted few, listen to the gifted few's music, use the gifted few's inventions and art, and read the poems, fantasies and plays by the gifted few.

This is what our education and culture conditions us to believe, and this is a culturally induced and perpetuated lie.

Building upon this lie, the dominant cultural élite tell us that the planning, design and building of any part of the environment is so difficult and so special that only the gifted few – those with degrees and certificates in planning, engineering, architecture, art, education, behavioural psychology, and so on – can properly solve environmental problems.

The result is that the vast majority of people are not allowed (and worse – feel that they are incompetent) to experiment with the components of building and construction, whether in environmental studies, the abstract arts, literature or science: the creativity – the playing around with the components and variables of the world in order to make experiments and discover new things and form new concepts – has been explicitly stated as the domain of the creative few, and the rest of the community has been deprived of a crucial part of their lives and lifestyle.

Within the architectural world there are people who are hammering out the implications of this approach: Habraken and Hertzberger in the Netherlands, Giancarlo de Carlo in Italy, the most recent generation of architectural students in Britain. Within the educational world there are people who have grasped its educational implications. For example, Dr Eric Midwinter in his report on the Educational Priority Area project in Liverpool, refers to what he calls the planners' lip-service to consultation, and says: "They may knock on the door of a client for rehabilitation or re-housing and ask what sort of home and environment is required. What is the unfortunate interviewee to say in answer to this? What in too many cases he could say is something like this, 'I was never educated to listen to that kind of question, nor to articulate responses, technical or creative, to it'."

This is why environmental education has to be an education that will enable people to become the masters of their own environment.

3. Towards a Poor School

The technological society has deliberately cultivated a careless, consumptive, egoistic and slovenly human being. The frugal society ... must start with redirecting our attitudes and re-educating our values – Henryk Skolimowski

Perhaps the best-known contribution made by John Dewey to the endless debate on education was his remark that "what the best and wisest parent wants for his own child, that must the community want for all of its children". But perhaps the best and wisest of parents are the very ones who are least able to specify their hopes in this respect, and the more they perceive and acknowledge the uniqueness of each child, the less likely would be their hopes for any particular child to have any general relevance. Unless, that is, they take refuge in generalities of universal application. They might want their child to be happy, to be fulfilled, to be autonomous, or to 'make a contribution'. But who doesn't? What guide to individual or collective action could we derive from such aspirations?

I have a friend, a Paraguayan anarchist, whose children were named according to parental convictions. Regardless of sex or custom, the first was named Liberty, the second was called Equality and the third was named Fraternity (if you are wondering what the fourth child of the family was called, I

Address to the Annual Conference of the Dartington Society, 22nd April 1977, published in the *New Humanist*, September/October 1977, and in Mark Braham (editor) *Aspects of Education* (Chichester: John Wiley, 1982).

have to tell you that he was called Ché). It is hard to guess which of the family would grow up most embarrassed by this imposition of ideology on nomenclature, and I have no idea whether he sought for each child an education compatible with the slogans with which he labelled his offspring. He would be in trouble if he did, because the resounding catch-phrases we have inherited from the eighteenth century may go marvellously together on French postage stamps, but do they go together in life, or in educational policy making? Dr Ronald Sampson of Bristol recently gave an address with the title 'The Choice Between Inequality and Freedom in Education' and that title at least draws attention to one of our most agonising and unresolved educational dilemmas.

For it often seems to me that people's social and political attitudes are determined not on the conventional left-right spectrum but on the relative values they place on at least the first two characters in this holy trinity. There is a quite different continuum which shapes their approaches to the politics of education as to everything else: that between authoritarians and libertarians. In terms of the ordinary crudities of party politics, you can, for example, place our representatives in either of the two main parties on this continuum, and you might very well find that in one of those two parties the egalitarians are always on the back benches, while in the other the libertarians are usually to be found there. In the politics of education in Britain, people's devotion to one or other of these principles leads them into some very sterile posturing, and it often lays them open to uncomfortable charges of hypocrisy since sometimes what they want for their own children is something other than what they want for all the community's children.

The pathos of the battle for equality in education is that it revolves around the principle of the quality of opportunity to be unequal. The last word on this particular issue was said many years ago in a deceptively modest little book, disguised as a satire, *The Rise of the Meritocracy* by Michael Young. This book looks back from the twenty-first century at our own day as the period when "two contradictory principles for legitimising power were struggling for mastery – the principle of kinship and the principle of merit". Kinship implies that you are the child of your parents and consequently have access to the opportunities they can provide. In Michael Young's satire, Merit wins in the end, with the perfection of intelligence testing, and consequently with earlier and earlier selection a new, non-self-perpetuating elite is formed consisting of the "five per cent of the population who know what five per cent means". The top jobs go to the top people, and Payment by Merit (M equals IQ plus Effort) widens the gap between top and bottom people. The people at the bottom not only are treated as inferior, they *know* they *are* inferior. But to select the few is to reject the many, and in the meritocratic society new tensions arise. By the end of the twentieth century, although the new working class no longer includes people of outstanding intellectual capacity (since they have all been creamed off by meritocratic selection), a populist movement arises consisting of dissident intellectuals, mainly women, allied with the disruptive proletariat, declaring in the Chelsea Manifesto of the year 2000 their belief in the classless society.

Needless to say, the manifesto cuts no ice with the meritocrats of the year 2000, though it becomes a rallying point in the bitter insurrection in 2033.

The Chelsea Manifesto declared that:

The classless society would be one which both possessed and acted upon plural values. Were we to evaluate people not according to their intelligence and their education, their occupation and their power, but according to their sympathy and generosity, there could be no classes. Who would be able to say that the scientist was superior to the porter with admirable qualities as a father, and the civil servant with unusual skill at gaining prizes superior to the lorry driver with unusual skill at growing roses? The classless society would also be the tolerant society, in which individual differences were actually encouraged as well as passively tolerated, in which full meaning was at last given to the dignity of man. Every human being would then have equal opportunity, not to rise up in the world in the light of any mathematical measure, but to develop his own special capacities for leading a rich life.

Well, my own experience is that the same people who would give an enthusiastic ideological assessment to the propositions of the Chelsea Manifesto complain most bitterly when they discover that their children can earn more working for the district council's cleansing department than they can in the lower ranks of professional employment; yet in the strike of toolroom workers at British Leyland in February 1977 they would bitterly criticise the strikers who asserted that with their years of training and immense skill they would only earn the same as foremen of the lavatory cleaners. Other people's defence of pay differentials is always marked by sordid self-interest: our own is always above reproach. Education is not a path to social equality.

What do we say about liberty, the first of the holy trinity? As a political issue this is construed as parental freedom of choice in schooling for their children. As an educational issue it means, among a great many other things, the absence of coercion of the child: the goods are displayed in the educational supermarket and the customer selects or rejects. I am afraid that, with the exception of a few heroes known by name to most of us, we are as guilty of hypocrisy in the name of this great abstraction as we are in the name of equality. In the publicly provided education system we have a book of martyrs to make the point, among them Mr Duane, Mr MacKenzie and Mr Ellis. In the privately provided sector we know how, at some stage in adolescence, parental interest in the sacred freedom of the child diminishes until the child is removed suddenly to attend a cramming establishment to achieve whatever educational qualifications are necessary to keep open the doors to a growing number of adult careers.

Martin Buber, looking into the candid eyes of a rebellious pupil, remarked "I love freedom, but I don't believe in it". His remark epitomises the position of the modern progressive parents. They do love freedom so long as it does not interfere with the chances of their children in the occupational status race. It is nothing to do with the education system or with the philosophy of education, but it is a fact that in most high-status jobs the qualifications for entry as well as the length of training have been raised and extended to a ludicrous extent in order to up-grade that occupation. I need only to mention one occupation, that with which I am most familiar, the profession of architecture. To be accepted for professional training involves at the outset, in terms of the English education system, three 'O' Levels and two 'A' Levels, preferably in approved subjects, followed by six years of professional training, after which the successful aspirant finds himself preparing schedules of doors and windows for some building in the design of which he has had no hand. Now within living memory – and I think you will probably agree that architecture has been of an aesthetically and technically higher standard within the lifespan of some living people – it was totally different. Sir Clough Williams-Ellis, who is still alive, confided to Sir Edwin Lutyens that he spent a term at the Architectural Association in London, learning his trade. "A term", said Lutyens, horrified. "My dear fellow, it took me three weeks". Was Lutyens a better or worse architect than the people who by a restrictive Act of Parliament are today exclusively entitled to call themselves architects? The first architect I ever worked for learned his trade at an age when we still by law imprison children in the compulsory education machine, drawing full-size details in chalk on brown paper on a barn floor here in Devon, for the building of Truro Cathedral for the man to whom he was apprenticed, Sir John Loughborough Pearson, RA. Go and look at the building and see if it leaks.

What I say of an occupation of which I have intimate knowledge applies, I am certain, to the whole range of employment. I deliberately mentioned various architectural knights to indicate that I am not generalising from the experience of the riff-raff of the architectural profession who all, no doubt, have been through the academic treadmill. In this I am saying, as in so many other spheres of life, professionalism is a conspiracy against the laity, and if it is the reason why we have tacitly abandoned our educational belief in liberty, we need to be quite clear that it is these external circumstances rather than our educational ideas which have forced us into this position.

For motivated families, the belief in liberty has been modified by the requirements of occupational entrance, and this view has spread from the intelligentsia to the skilled working class. Anyone from a city like Glasgow, Newcastle or Belfast will tell you how the educational qualifications for an engineering apprenticeship have risen to impossible heights within the last

decade. You need two 'O' Levels to be employed with a
car-washing machine in South Shields. No doubt you
occasionally wash the cars lent by the Department of
Education and Science to members of Her Majesty's
Inspectorate so that they can get around to schools and tell
teachers about the need to encourage children to aim at jobs
in Britain's manufacturing industries.

Poor families and poor children interpret liberty in education
quite differently. When the sociology graduate from Keele
University drifts into teaching because we are overstocked
with sociologists, and announces to his class that he wants
them to feel free to express their own view of the situation,
those amongst his conscripts who can actually hear his voice
conclude with resignation that he does not really care about
them. They conclude that in his opinion they are not worth
teaching, and in their minds this is why he adopts his
laissez-faire attitude. 'He didn't care whether we learned
anything or not' is their verdict on the now-departed teacher.
We have written off liberty as an educational goal.

What are we to say about fraternity as one of the aims of
education? It is a concept even harder to define than the other
two. Looking for a way of coming to terms with the idea, I am
helped by a passage I read recently from André Malraux's
book *Lazare*. He says:

> People think they understand Fraternity because they confuse it with human
> warmth. But in point of fact it is something much deeper, and it was
> belatedly, and almost apologetically, that it was added to the blazon of the
> Republic, whose flag at first bore only the words Liberty and Equality ...
> The word Liberty has still the same ring to it, but Fraternity now stands
> only for a comical utopia in which nobody would ever have a bad character.
> Men believe that Fraternity was just tacked on, one Sunday, to feelings like
> Justice and Liberty. But it is not something that can be tacked on at will. It
> is something sacred, and it will elude us if we rob it of the irrational element
> that lies hidden within it. It is as mysterious as love, it has nothing to do
> with duty, or with 'right thinking'. Like love, and unlike liberty, it is a
> provisional sentiment, a state of grace.

I am sure that Malraux betrays some ignorance of the history
of ideas in his own country in making these remarks, but that
is not my concern. Can we get closer to the meaning of
fraternity? Peter Kropotkin chose to define it as 'mutual aid'

and in his book of that name he remarks that:

> To reduce animal sociability to *love* and *sympathy* means to reduce its generality and its importance, just as human ethics based on love and personal sympathy only have contributed to narrow the comprehension of the moral feeling as a whole. It is not love of my neighbour – whom I often do not know at all – which induces me to seize a pail of water and to rush towards his house when I see it on fire; it is a far wider, even though more vague feeling or instinct of human solidarity and sociability which moves me ... It is a feeling infinitely wider than love or personal sympathy – an instinct that has been slowly developed among animals and men in the course of an extremely long evolution, and which has taught animals and men alike the force they can borrow from the practice of mutual aid and support, and the joys they can find in social life.

Well, he's right, isn't he? But when the sense of fraternity, or solidarity, is cultivated in educational institutions it is frequently in opposition to the institution itself. Teachers know that the fraternity is that of the peer group and that the values it represents are profoundly anti-educational. "I have the greatest difficulty in restraining them from tearing up each other's work at the end of the period", a hard-pressed secondary school teacher told me. Indeed, the closer we get to the classroom, the more diminished is our faith that the school can be the agent of social change or the vehicle for social justice. In many parts of the world there is still a hunger for schooling. Immense sacrifices are made by parents to achieve it for their children. They and their children would find unbelievable the size of education budgets in the schools of the Western world and the low esteem in which our schools are held by their scholars.

Thirteen years ago I wrote an article called 'A Modest Proposal for the Repeal of the Education Act', and it was later blessed in the symposium 'Children's Rights' as "the first time anyone in England had dared to formulate out loud, even to a possibly friendly audience, what many of us had begun to hear as a question in our heads". That reference to a friendly audience is important because it is easy to be misunderstood. At a time when teachers are joining the ranks of the unemployed, and when their unions as well as those of students are demonstrating under banners reading 'Fight the Education Cuts', am I not grotesquely misjudging the present

climate of education in putting on my banner the slogan
'Towards a Poor School'?

Let me declare my vested interest in having rich schools. I
earn half my living producing a bulletin for teachers called
BEE, the Bulletin of Environmental Education. It costs £4 a year
– a modest sum – and in the last year the curve of circulation
growth has completely flattened, as our renewal notices keep
getting returned with sad little notes saying 'We like it very
much. It's marvellously useful, but we have had to cut our
spending drastically'. I always say that they ought to ask their
classes to subscribe their pennies on the grounds that getting
our bulletin will improve the quality of the teaching they are
subjected to, but no one takes me seriously because it is a basic
educational principle, isn't it, that no one should raise a penny
for his own education?

I earn the other half of my income running a project for the
Schools Council, which is the body concerned with
curriculum development in England and Wales. Our project
is called 'Art and the Built Environment'. Can you imagine
anything more frivolous, while the nation's economy goes
down the drain? Not only is our project one of those marginal
frills, by the standards of the education industry, but its
sponsor, the Schools Council, is itself vulnerable. The
notorious Yellow Paper – the report to the Prime Minister
from the Department of Education and Science, which was
leaked to the press – described its performance as "mediocre".
So I have a strong interest in an education system rich enough
to support marginal activities – or activities which in the eyes
of the system are marginal.

In what sense do I see virtues in the idea of a poor school?
There is a Polish stage producer, Grotowski, who wrote a book
called *Towards a Poor Theatre*, implying that the theatre would
get a new lease of life if it shed all the expensive trimmings of
the proscenium, elaborate lighting and equipment: all that
audio-visual gear. (Actually there is a parallel in school here.
Do any of our great drama teachers – people like Dorothy
Heathcote in Newcastle, for example – have any use for the
elaborate theatre equipment with which many schools
encumbered themselves in the days when we thought we were

rich?) Similarly there is a movement, as I understand it, in the Christian church known as 'Towards a Poor Church', a kind of echo of all those religious performers who have haunted that religion, with their bare feet and shaggy beards, urging their fellows to abandon all that expensive architecture and ecclesiastical silverware in order to free themselves to become receptive to the Message. (Actually there is a parallel in school here, too, with those earnest members of the Church of England who think that the only thing that can save the church is disestablishment – the severing of its official connection with the state. Many teachers of what we call religious education in school believe that the only thing that can save the reputation of their subject – which in this country is the only school subject established by law and at the same time the only one we can opt our children out of – is the ending of its statutory existence as well as that of the common act of worship which is supposed to take place in morning assembly.)

Whatever we may say when we lobby against cuts in educational spending, let us reflect between friends on the implications of educational poverty. And before we get self-righteous about it, let us think about the implications of the Houghton pay award to teachers a couple of years go. Cause and effect there may or may not be, but before Houghton, when teachers were complaining about their poverty, there was no job shortage, there was a teacher shortage. Many schools had a terrifying turnover of staff every term. In 1974 many urban schools were sending children home because there was no one to teach them. I read two items about the same city in the same newspaper on the same day that year, one of which reported the sending home of schoolchildren for this reason while the other reported the rounding-up by the police of truants, collected off the streets. After the Houghton pay award, the huge staff turnover stopped: the oldest inhabitants of the city school became the staff once more instead of the fifth-year conscripts, and the supply of jobs dried up. As the schools became poorer, they became more stable as institutions.

The truth is that in the boom period, now over, education was oversold. Every additional bit of expenditure, every increase in student numbers at the upper and more expensive end of the system, every new development in educational technology, was a step towards some great social goal. But it has not delivered the goods. Professor A.H. Halsey, writing in *The Times Educational Supplement* (21st January 1977), remarks that:

We live today under sentence of death by a thousand cuts (that is, of all things except the body of bureaucracy). In education the position is one of extreme relative deprivation, not only because of the financial background of a sudden halt to previously mounting largesse, but also, and more seriously, because of the collapse of *belief* in education, either as the best investment for national production, or the great redistributor of chances to the traditionally disadvantaged.

Nor is this simply a British phenomenon. Fred M. Hechinger, the author of *Growing Up in America*, also writing in *The Times Educational Supplement* (5th November 1976), says that "America is in headlong retreat from its commitment to education. Political confusion and economic uncertainty have shaken the people's faith in education as the key to financial and social success". Among these people or trends which he blames for this changed circumstance are the right-wing backlash and what he calls the "destructive" influence of the deschoolers like Ivan Illich and the views of critics like Edgar Z. Friedenberg, John Holt and Christopher Jencks. I think, on the contrary, that these people have had an immensely liberatory effect on our ideas about the way that the intelligentsia lapped up the deschooling literature of a few years ago – the works of Paul Goodman, Everett Reimer and Ivan Illich – but when, at the same time, the schools were sending home pupils for lack of teachers, they failed, with a few exceptions in the 'free school' movement, to make the connection. The community did not seize the occasion to use the wonderful resources of the city to provide an alternative education for the kids who were wandering the streets. They just waited for the statistics for such offences as shoplifting, vandalism and taking-and-driving-away, to rise – which they did. At the same time in the universities, well-educated Marxist lecturers were explaining how the education system in our society was simply a device for preparing us for our particular slot in capitalist industry. The government, as though anxious to prove them right, has set off a moral panic about the failure of the education system to meet the needs of industry.

My friend, Stan Cohen, wrote a book about the shaping of stereotypes in the public mind on such themes as 'mods', 'rockers', 'skinheads' and 'greasers', and gave it the title *Folk Devils and Moral Panics*. I would extrapolate from that title the notion that whenever you have a moral panic you have to find a folk devil. We have a moral panic about the state of education, so we find a folk devil in all those soft options that the kids are fiddling around with instead of bashing away at literacy and numeracy and getting ready for the world of work. This particular moral panic was set off by a speech from the Prime Minister, but the process that Cohen calls media amplification has been at work, so that what he actually said was considerably less denunciatory than the accompanying chorus off-stage. When Mr Callaghan made his speech at Ruskin College, enormous attention was focused on the occasion. This was not because of the nice irony that that particular college was founded to give a liberal education to working men, thus ensuring that they would never go back to what Eric Gill called the "subhuman condition of intellectual irresponsibility" to which we condemn industrial workers, but because of the leak to the press in the previous week of that Yellow Paper – the document prepared by the Department of Education and Science to brief the Prime Minister – which swiped away at all the sacred cows of education except, of course, the Department of Education and Science and Her Majesty's Inspectorate. I must say that I found nothing objectionable about the Prime Minister's speech, but I cannot help feeling both cynicism and anger at the timing of this particular moral panic.

Is it because the government feels conscious that the rival party seems to be stealing its thunder in the public discussion of education? Or is it part of a smokescreen to divert attention from the fact that the cash is running out of the budgets of local education authorities? Well, never mind chaps, let's concentrate on the basics. It's back to 1870, the year of the

Act of Parliament which made schooling free, universal and compulsory, and also the year which marked the beginning of Britain's industrial decline. 1870? Well, just ask an economic historian. Isn't the educational industry, in fact, just the latest scapegoat for the state of the British economy?

The Prime Minister in his Ruskin speech said that he wanted to open a national debate on education, and remarked that "the debate that I was seeking has got off to a flying start even before I was able to say anything". Too true. I found it hilarious to learn from *The Guardian* on 14th October 1976 – the week *before* Mr Callaghan's speech – that "a multi-million pound emergency programme to monitor standards in primary and secondary schools has been started by the DES", just at the time when the schools themselves are being obliged to make multi-million pound cuts in their own spending, and just when education committees are solemnly debating reducing the calorific value of schools meals as well as raising the price of them. Professor Halsey was absolutely right in suggesting that the last thing that would be cut was the educational bureaucracy. I read that week in the Sunday papers that the Welsh Secretary, Mr John Morris, has also pre-empted the result of the debate by giving "clear uncompromising guidance ... circulated to every head teacher in the Principality", saying that "the priority must be tilted towards the engineer, the scientist and the mathematician. And in addition our children must be taught the languages of Europe to such a degree of proficiency that they can sell and service our products in the countries of our trading partners".

I am deeply suspicious of all this talk. I do not believe that the roots of or the cure for our chronic economic malaise are to be found in the education system and, if it is true that the young do not like industrial jobs, either a shopfloor or a graduate level (and it is symptomatic of the superficial nature of the debate that it fails to distinguish between the two), I think it ironical that instead of wanting to change the nature of industrial work, of wanting to make it an adventure instead of a penance, we should want to change the nature of the young. Actually it is not even true that we are short of graduate engineers and we are certainly not short of shop-floor fodder.

There must be many teachers who went through the boom years without even knowing that they were in them: they found themselves committed to a policy of make-do-and-mend as usual, and never got their hands on the money because it was being spent somewhere else. No one here who is a teacher will deny my assertion that the characteristic situation is for the teacher to say all year that he would like this or that set of books or piece of equipment and be told that there was no cash, while three days before the end of the financial year the head of department would say 'you've got four hundred pounds to spend by the end of the week. Let me know what to order before the end of the afternoon because otherwise we'll lose the money'. I was in a school the other day, in an art and design department, where thousands of pounds were available to spend on machinery, but the art teacher had only £38 to lay out on paper, paint and other expendables. He could have kilns but no clay. As an advocate of the use of the local environment in education, I have often come across the situation where the teacher can easily get an illuminated terrestrial globe to suspend from the ceiling, but found that it was not in order for him to buy a class set of street maps for the locality.

One of the ways in which hierarchical systems work is by withholding information on the budget. We see this at a national level where the Chancellor of the Exchequer has it all in his black box to reveal to a waiting nation on budget day. Secrecy is made into a fetish and politicians have been disgraced because of budget leaks. But should not the nation's budget be the subject of earnest discussion throughout the country for months before? It is the same with the education budget and the budget of the school itself. I am willing personally to join in the scramble for slices of the diminishing cake, but which group of supplicants, all shouting 'me too', do I join? This is what is happening at the ludicrously stage-managed regional conferences being held by the DES and the ministers around the country, where every kind of special and sectional interest is being given the opportunity to say 'me too'.

I would rather join a different campaign. My bit of graffiti

would say 'open the books'. Just what is the school's budget
and how is it to be allocated? What subject interest is starved
just because it does not use a lot of prestige equipment? Just
what is the authority's budget and how much of that goes in
administration? Just what is the nation's education budget and
how much of it is spent by the DES on itself? A year ago, John
Vaizey, in one of his provocative little contributions to the
education press, asked "Do we really need the DES?" Exactly
what function, he asked, has the department, when the local
authorities themselves have inspectors and subject advisers,
and when we have a theoretically decentralised education
system? Her Majesty's inspectors are always blandly telling us
that they have no control over the curriculum. If you took a
conspiratorial view of politics you might think that the Yellow
Paper is the department's attempt to assert, in the face of Lord
Vaizey (who is, after all, one of our foremost authorities on
the economics of education), that it *has* a function, or is going
to make one for itself.

Some people will remember a frivolous little book called
Parkinson's Law, whose author commented, among other
things, that as the Navy had fewer and fewer ships the
Admiralty had more and more employees. Much more
recently there is the instance of the National Health Service,
which is the largest single employer in Britain. In the ten years
before its reorganisation, its staff increased by 65 per cent. Its
medical staff, however, increased during this period by 21 per
cent, and its domestic staff by 2 per cent. The truth is,
unpalatable as it must be for those people who believe in
government action and government funding for every task
which society has to fulfil, that the governmental mechanism
develops a momentum of its own: it secures and guarantees
its own future. You will have seen photographs in the papers
(e.g. *The Sunday Times*, 6th March 1977) of the new office
blocks for the administrators and the old Nissen huts for the
patients, and you will have read that the staff of the
consultants, McKinsey's, who advised on the reorganisation
of the Health Service two years ago, now believe that they gave
the wrong advice. You may have heard on the radio Mr Tatton
Brown, who was chief architect for the Department of Health

from 1959 to 1971, reflecting that the advice he and his colleagues gave to the Regional Health Authorities was not the right advice on hospital design. As you know, the pundits of hospital organisation were advising the closing of those little local hospitals in favour of huge regional complexes like Addenbrooke's and Northwick Park. Now suddenly they have swung around to praising the local cottage hospital as being manageable, friendly, community-oriented and economic. But the machine they set in motion is still condemning local hospitals to death. There is an exact parallel in school planning. A series of obsolete assumptions about the size of the sixth form generated the idea of the huge unmanageable comprehensive school, and the rationalising out of existence of small secondary schools is still in process, long after any teacher believes that there is anything to be gained from doing so, just as the war against selective secondary schools is still being fought long after we have given up the hope that the education system can be used to promote social justice.

The person who worships the state and thinks that any other model of provision is a let-off for the state or a cop-out from the state, when faced by the politics of retrenchment, can only protest and wave his banner. There is, for example, in the world of pre-school education a deep ideological division between those who believe in the provision of day nurseries and nursery schools by local education authorities, on principle, and those who believe on principle in babyminders and parent-organised playgroups. Every now and then there is a scandal about illicit babyminding, but it was left to an outsider, Brian Jackson, to think up the idea of courses in babyminding for unofficial babyminders. Now, as part of its education cuts, one English county has decided, reluctantly, to close all its nursery schools. The customers are helpless. If the local community had developed its own unofficial network of provision for the under-fives, it would have been better off today.

I was walking through a country town the other day when I passed a building with that little-red-schoolhouse look and, sure enough, there was a stone let into the wall saying: "These two classrooms were built by public subscription on the occasion of the coronation of King Edward VII, 1901". Well, I am not enthusiastic about commemorating him or his descendants, but I do think that in education as in many other fields of life we have thrown away a huge fund of energy, goodwill and popular involvement, in abandoning the principle of voluntary self-taxation to improve facilities, in the name of universal publicly provided facilities. Dependence on government means that we become powerless when some centralised decision-making system says, according to priorities which may be wise or foolish, that we are not going to get what we want through the system. The rediscovery of the voluntary ethic can happen quite quickly: I read earlier this year that parents from the Sussex villages of Ferring and Findon have offered to put up two prefabricated classrooms at Angmering Comprehensive School, because the extra classrooms have been axed by government spending cuts. The *Evening News* (7th January 1977) says that the council's schools committee has recommended that West Sussex County Council accepts the 'revolutionary' idea. As I have indicated, the idea is not all that revolutionary. In the poor world, it would be taken for granted. Illiterate poor parents in the shanty towns on the fringe of a Latin American city would take it for granted that they should build a primary school for their children. However, one of the cuts that Essex County Council has decided on is that no further swimming instruction or maintenance should be provided in pools run by parent-teacher associations. Now that really is a foolish gesture because it will deter other parent-teacher associations from providing swimming pools. The council should have leant over backwards to fulfil its part of the bargain, just to show how valuable it thought parent and teacher initiatives are.

In the situation of a 'no-growth' economy, which to my mind is our situation today and which we are faced with in any conceivable future, there are certain priorities which are self-evident to me. I find, to my horror and amazement, that they are all totally revolutionary. My first priority is that we should put our money at the bottom end of education rather than at the top. Now this really would be a revolutionary change in the order of things. For the greater sums of money that are poured into the education industries of the world, the smaller the proportion which benefits the people at the bottom of the educational, occupational and social hierarchy. The universal system turns out to be yet another way in which the poor are obliged to subsidise the rich. A decade ago, Everett Reimer found that the children of the poorest one-tenth of the population of the United States cost the public in schooling $2,500 each over a lifetime, while the children of the richest one-tenth cost about $35,000. "Assuming that one-third of this is private expenditure, the richest one-tenth still gets ten times as much of public funds for education as the poorest one-tenth." In his suppressed UNESCO report of 1970, Michael Huberman reached the same conclusion for the majority of countries in the world. In Britain we spend twice as much on the secondary school life of a grammar school sixth former as on a secondary modern school leaver, while, if we include university expenditure, we spend as much on an undergraduate in one year as on a normal school child throughout his life. The Fabian tract *Labour and Inequality* calculates that "while the highest social group benefit seventeen times as much as the lowest group from the expenditure on universities, they only contribute five times as much revenue". No wonder Everett Reimer calls schools an almost perfectly regressive form of taxation. In the scramble for dwindling public expenditure on education, you may be sure that the universities are going to be almost obscenely successful by comparison with the pre-school education lobby.

In re-ordering our expenditure, I would invest heavily in pre-school education, and in the infant and junior school. My aim would be the traditional, and currently approved one, that every child should be literate and numerate on leaving the junior school at 11. All right, it will take up to the age of 14 to achieve this for some children, but I want to assert that the compulsory prolongation of schooling beyond such an age is an affront to the freedom of the individual and has nothing to do with the aims of education, even though it has everything to do with the restrictive practices of the job market. I mentioned earlier the entry qualifications demanded by the architectural profession. A month ago the RIBA Council solemnly sat and discussed how to make it harder still – like demanding four 'A' Levels – so as to restrict entry still further. Do we have to wait until two 'A' Levels instead of two 'O' Levels are needed to get a carwash job in South Shields, or do we say enough is enough: this is not what we have teachers for?

I quoted earlier the brilliant satire *The Rise of the Meritocracy*, written by Michael Young in the 1950s. He was interviewed by one of the Sunday papers this year and explained why he feels that there is no future for secondary schools as we know them. He said:

I think secondary schools in their present form are doomed. They haven't yet managed to reflect the new kind of family. The father used to be the fount of authority. Today, that authority is greatly diminished partly because it's shared. Schools and universities borrowed authority from the authoritarian father and now that it's no longer there to be borrowed, children in secondary schools are not going to accept it. There has to be a reduction in the school-leaving age and a move over to half-time education. People will be learning at home, at the workplace and not forced into institutions which use a bogus authority.

Dr Young has the honesty and the poor taste to bring up the subject of the crisis of authority in the secondary school: a crisis that ensures that much of our expenditure on teachers and plant is wasted by attempting to teach people what they do not want to learn in a situation that they would rather not be involved in. A poor school could not afford such waste and frustration of both teachers and taught. The school has become one of the instruments by which we exclude adolescents from real responsibilities and real functions in the life of our society. We have in the last year of secondary schooling pathetic attempts to give 'relevance' by providing 'work experience' courses aimed at acclimatising the young to the shock of going to work, or by providing courses in colleges of further education with such titles as 'Adjustment to Work', for the benefit of those unable or unwilling to hold down a job. The Trades Union Congress and the Confederation of British Industry have joined forces in backing a project for informing schoolchildren about industry. Arthur Young, the headmaster of Northcliffe High School in Yorkshire, has for years been trying to find the right equation between learning and earning. He values the efforts of his pupils to earn money for themselves and has sought, within the narrow prescribed limits of the law, to provide opportunities in and out of school for them to do so. He remarks of work experience projects that they:

have never really got off the ground because of the legal, insurance and trade union problems that hedge them around. I have always thought that the schemes proposed were phoney – the most important aspect of work experience is being neglected completely – the wage at the end of the week.

Like Michael Young, Arthur Young sees an urgent need to change the relationships in the secondary school. Describing the efforts made to provide actual cash-earning experiences for the most unlikely lads at his school, and the effect it has had on their attitudes to running their own lives, taking decisions, budgeting, fulfilling obligations, dealing with strangers, as well as such mundane things taken for granted by the middle-class child as using the telephone, he remarks:

We have to overcome the ridiculous idea that giving children the chance to earn money in school is somehow immoral ... In the changing situation in education, pupil-teacher relationships and roles are the essence of much heart-searching and debate. We might do well to compare the differences in an earning-learning situation between master and apprentice and in the traditional school situation, captive scholars facing chalk and talk across the barrier of the teacher's desk. The comparison of relationships between newsagent and paperboy and between paperboy and schoolmaster might also be revealing.

The carelessly rich school, greedy for resources, has no need to be a productive institution. The poor school could not afford not to be a productive workshop and belongs to a society in which every workshop is an effective school. Don't think I am denigrating or down-grading the teacher. Far from it. A poor school could not afford to have its spending kept out of the individual teacher's hands. A poor school needs to know what it is paying for. In the 1960s educational spenders were swept away on a tide of commercially inspired expensive options like programmed learning and teaching machines, which are greeted with a cynical laugh in the 1970s. The expensive hardware of educational technology has become an irrelevancy and an embarrassment in this decade. I want the school to have a clearly stated published budget with a personal allocation to each member of the staff to spend as he or she sees fit. The teacher should be responsible for his own spending. He can do it wisely or foolishly on such materials and equipment as he desires. He can pool it with others, he can carry it over to next year.

The poor school would be self-catering. Why shouldn't the school meals service be in the hands of the pupils? Why shouldn't every secondary school include a day nursery run by the pupils? The poor school would be too valuable a community asset to be open for a small part of the day and for a restricted age band. Already we are feeling our way towards such an institution through the concept of the community school and the community college. When we consider how little the massive educational spending of the last decade did to enhance the lives or life-chances of the children in what is known as 'the lower quartile of the ability range' in secondary education, we may perhaps hope that the new age of frugality will lead us to devise appropriate educational experiences in a climate where we make fewer grandiose claims for what the school can do. By settling for less, we might even achieve more.

4. How Can I Use the Environment in my Teaching?

Whatever my intentions, I only find myself in Glasgow once or twice a year, and when I am, kind friends here usually take me to see some place or activity which I will find interesting or encouraging. Jim Johnson, of this university, will take me to see the work of the community-based housing associations, promoted with the intention of devolving control of resources for rehabilitation down to a local level so that the community could set its own standards and organise its own work. Or friends in the Education Department, or in the Department of Education, will take me to a school where something new is happening in the field of environmental education.

If you have read the opening pages of my book *The Child in the City* you may recall that I describe such a visit, made several years ago now, to a particular district of the city where a continuous programme of redevelopment by the Corporation has been in progress for years. There were three-storey walk-up flats built in the years just before the war, more built in the post-war years, as well as the tower block of the last decade. And there were some of the remaining traditional Glasgow tenement houses of four or five storeys, some still occupied, some being demolished at the moment. In the middle of the area I arrived at the shabby premises of the Free School, run by a teacher with the impeccable academic qualifications demanded by the Scottish education system

Lecture at the conference of the Scottish Committee for Environmental Education, Glasgow, 10th March 1979.

who chose to use his talents in this alternative institution
because he had lost faith in the official system. He was,
needless to say, in trouble with the local education authority
because the old building he occupied did not comply with the
regulations as to the appropriate number of lavatories for each
sex. Opposite his school, emerging from the ground, was the
structure of the vast new secondary school which would
combine the existing schools of the area.

But will this new building mean that either the unofficial
community school or the truancy centre (or 'intermediate
school for casual attenders' run by a remarkable priest in
association with one of the existing secondary schools) will no
longer be needed? An official report by the Scottish Education
Department's inspectors on the effect of raising the school
leaving age suggests the opposite, and declares frankly that the
schools had ignored the needs of less able pupils in favour of
examination courses with the result that many pupils became
disenchanted and simply stayed away.

Just round the corner was the new primary school. It was a
brand new building, open-plan, carpeted, quiet, civilised and,
even in these hard times in the education industry, amply
stocked with all the attractive paraphernalia of junior teaching,
although the first thing the Corporation had to do once it had
taken over the building was to fit wire grilles to doors and
windows and arrange for security men with dogs to do their
night patrols once the janitor had gone off duty. The
headmistress was quite obviously one of those marvels of the
teaching profession, efficient, tough-minded and
tender-hearted, who had first taught in the district twenty
years earlier. I asked her what differences she perceived
between those days and now. She replied that when she first
taught there she had noticed among the children the effects
of poor feeding, poor clothing, scabies, impetigo, nits, dental
decay and ringworm. And she said that today it was just the
same except for the absence of ringworm.

I asked whether she could discern a difference between the
families in the old tenement blocks and those in the relatively
new corporation flats. She replied that in the old tenement
blocks there tended to be families who were in work, who

remained as a family unit and who paid their rent. Perhaps it would be true to say that in that particular district everybody with the ability to get out had got out, and the perfectly sanitary corporation flats there (which incidentally looked to me to have had no real attention to maintenance since they were built) had become the homes of the lame ducks of official policy who had not the ability to move out. The families in the notorious old tenements opted *not* to move there.

The secondary school headmaster said much the same. It was curious, he thought, that those parents who still lived in the old 'single-end' tenements with the sink on the landing and the 'cludgie' on the common stair, would send their children to school cleaner and better nourished than those from the post-war flats which at least provided those facilities which the Medical Officer of Health regarded as essential for the good life.

These are unpalatable observations for those who hold to the faith of the social engineering professions that bigger and better schools or bigger and better units of housing or more expert and intensive social work will modify the culture of poverty. When I met Roger Starr, the Housing Administrator for New York, whose problems make those of Sheffield and Glasgow seem like minor local difficulties, he asked rhetorically: "To what extent can government intervene to change *people*? Should a concern for human welfare drive government itself to impose specific behavioural patterns on those who are neither certifiably insane nor provably guilty of a criminal offence?" The British government's answer has been clearly stated (on paper at least). Reporting to the 1976 United Nations Conference on the Human Habitat on its various palliative experiments in deprived inner city areas, like Urban Aid and the Community Development Projects, it declares that they "have confirmed beyond doubt that the inner city's decline results from an external economic process, not from any change in the behaviour patterns of the inhabitants".

Looking at the experience of the city from the point of view of its child inhabitants, I think there is another factor: the scope and limits of one's own actions. During the period of mushroom growth in the cities of Britain and America in the nineteenth century, you get the impression that the child always had something to do, something to engage him in the experience of living. It is easy to see that he usually had too much to do: that he had to consider himself lucky to work for intolerable hours at some dreary labour which was beyond his strength and earned a pittance. Or that he was engaged in a desperate struggle to get food for himself and his family. But he was not trapped in a situation where there was nothing economically rational for him to do and where his whole background and culture prevented him from benefiting from the expensively provided education machine, beyond the tender atmosphere of the infant school.

The child who grows up in the poverty belt of the British or American city today is caught in a cage in which there is not even the illusion of freedom of action to change his situation, except of course in activities outside the law. Self-confidence and purposeful self-respect drain away from these children as they grow up because there is no way which makes sense to them, of becoming involved, except in a predatory way, in their own city. Sometimes there are glimpses which show the way towards another kind of involvement. When I mentioned to Roger Starr the instance of 'The Renigades', a Spanish-American teenage gang who had been entrusted with the rehabilitation of a landlord-abandoned apartment house in New York, he groaned. He was the man who had to authorise the bills. But was this not an instance of giving the young real responsibilities and opportunities which would give them a place in the city? The Glasgow priest who runs the truancy centre remarked that the last thing which his pupils (or the pupils of the school whose drop-outs he caters for) regard as important is a job – or indeed the very idea of going to work. Partly for the very obvious reason that in that decaying city with its decaying economy, the jobs do not exist, but partly, according to the secondary school headmaster, that so large a proportion of his pupils belong to families totally dependent on welfare handouts that there is no model to emulate.

But he told me in the next breath that when another of the

old tenement houses fell to the demolition contractor's ball and chain, the cry would go up 'tenny doon!' and the boys would hire a horse and cart, for £5 a day, and collect whatever metal was sticking out of the pile of rubble and sell it to the scrap metal merchants. In spite of the fact that the lead flashings, gutters and pipework had already been garnered by the professional lead-thieves, the priest told me that the boys were usually agreeably surprised at how much they could earn this way.

"I'm not saying they *should* be doing this", he said, but I could see that he admired them and was concerned with the existential value of childhood experiences. And sure enough, as I was being ferried back to the city centre in a Scottish Education Department car (they happen to be the same make and colour as the ones used by Glasgow CID) we kept passing and being re-passed by a horse and cart with four boys and a nosebag aboard. They looked at us, not apprehensively but with curiosity, as they got through the traffic jams more rapidly.

They were between 12 and 14 years old. They knew how to get hold of, and manipulate in dense traffic, a horse-drawn vehicle, and how to pilot it through the city to some entrepreneur who had a market for the last of the metallic rubbish of the old inner city.

Reflecting on this incident in my book, I commented that, like the gypsies (called an "important element" in the metal recovery industry by the chairman of the British Scrap Federation), they were part of an industry with an estimated turnover of way over a hundred million pounds, saving twice that sum in foreign exchange. Were they, I asked, the final generation of children who actually had an economic function in the inner city?

At least those boys had learned how to manipulate the city. Many children do not. This is not just a Glasgow issue, of course. A survey of children under five in the Handsworth district of Birmingham found that just under half *never* went out to play. "They have no access, either exclusive or shared, to play spaces at the front of back of the house and their parents feared for their safety if they let them out".

Describing an infants' school in Islington in North London, Sue Cameron remarks that: "The experience of many of these children during the first five years of their lives has been so limited that they come to school like so many blank pages. Near the school is a park and a busy Underground station, but many of the children have never been inside the park and some of them don't know what a tube train looks like. Asked what they did at the weekend, they usually say they just stayed at home." Even when we assume that they *must* have been around by the time they reach thirteen or fourteen, we find that such children's world is fantastically restricted. Teachers in a school on a housing estate in Bristol told me of the shock with which they learned that some of their teenage pupils had never been to the centre of the city. Teachers in the London borough of Brent told me of 13 and 14 year olds who had never seen the Thames; teachers in the boroughs of Lambeth and Southwark, in schools a few hundred yards from the river, told me of pupils who had never crossed it.

A decade ago Charles Hannam and his colleagues at the school of education of Bristol University set in motion an experiment in out-of-school education for what we then called the fourth year leavers in the city's secondary schools. They reported their work in a distinguished book, *Young Teachers and Reluctant Learners*, which described how their student teachers were each given an afternoon a week with two or three young people in their final year at school who had rejected everything that school stood for. Often the student teachers, who were as shy and uncertain with these boys and girls as the latter were with them, found that they were introducing their charges, for the first time, to some of the excitements and delights of the city. Apart from the lessons implicit for the young teachers, the reluctant learners were gaining some slight insight into what the city held for them: aspects of urban life taken for granted by children from wealthier or more sophisticated families.

A much more recent study from the same city, *In and Out of School* by Roger White and David Brockington, describes a logical extension to Hannam's work. The authors remark that "children who have experienced ten years of a compulsory system that has channelled and labelled them as failures are not going to jump for joy at the prospect of an extended sentence". Their Community Education Project was an attempt to provide, for a day and a half a day a week, an alternative educational experience, based upon a club staffed by trainee teachers and social workers. One of the members of the club was Bill Lawson, and the authors explain his predicament thus:

On the day Bill spent at the project instead of travelling with his mates from school, he would come straight home in the morning. Like all the others in the group Bill could claim a refund from school for the bus fare to the club. Yet though Bill's house was over two miles from us he always walked. On wet days he would arrive completely soaked (since he possessed no waterproof coat) and often shivering with cold. In reply to our questioning why he hadn't caught the bus, Bill would merely retort that he liked walking. But towards the end of the Christmas term, as the weather grew colder and predictably wetter, Bill's arrival time became increasingly later and more sporadic. After two morning in a row when he hadn't turned up (and we were assured by his mates that he wasn't ill or on holiday) one of us called in at his house after work. Bill was out, but his mum was at home. Had Bill given up coming because he was bored? 'Oh no', reassured his mum, 'he really enjoys going to club, but when it's wet he doesn't like walking all that way'. At the suggestion that Bill should catch the bus on rainy days, she smiled. 'It's no good; you see Bill walks because he doesn't know where to get off the bus at the other end and he won't ask the conductor'. Bill had lived in Bristol for all of his fifteen years. He had never seemed to us particularly introverted or shy. Indeed, if the reports from his mates were to be believed, he led a pretty wild social life with girls, pubs and discos. And yet he wouldn't ask a stranger the way to us.

It would be presumptuous to claim that there is a 'solution' to the problem of the isolation and alienation of a significant proportion of the city's children, or that more spending on play spaces and on playgroups, desirable as these are, provide the answer. It is quite certain that environmental education as a school activity is not a trendy fad but an essential compensatory device in trying to make the city observable and negotiable for its young. It is not a subject but an aspect of every kind of school subject, pressed into service to attempt to make children the masters rather than the victims of their environment. As just one example: Bob Pugh, as head of physical education at Peckham Manor School, adapted the sport of orienteering to the streets of South London just to make his pupils at home in their own city.

So far as play facilities are concerned, one thing that observation of the behaviour of children makes clear, though it has only recently entered the enormous literature of children's play and has yet to affect environmental policies, is that children will play everywhere and with anything. A city that is really concerned with the needs of its young will make the whole environment accessible to them. Park and playground designers who usurp the creative capacities of the very children who are intended to use their work by building play sculptures instead of providing the materials for children to make their own, or who have earnest conferences about the appropriate kind of fencing to use, should pause and think about the implications of Joe Benjamin's remark that "ideally there should be no fence; but when we reach that happy state we will have no need for adventure playgrounds". For the fenced-off child ghetto sharpens the division between the worlds of adults and children, while Benjamin's whole case is that we should share the same world. "The point is that the streets, the local service station, the housing estate stairway, indeed anything our urban community offers, is part of the natural habitat of the child. Our problem is not to design streets, housing, a petrol station or shops that can lend themselves to play, but to educate society to accept children on a participating basis". This explains why it was possible for Dennis Woods of North Carolina State University to deliver a paper with the title 'Free the Children! Down with Playgrounds!'

Hermann Mattern of Berlin underlines his point. "One should be able to play everywhere, loosely, and not be forced into a 'playground' or 'park'. The failure of an urban environment can be measured in direct proportion to the number of 'playgrounds'." Such an approach, of course, could easily be seized upon as a justification for *not* adapting the city parks to the needs of contemporary citizens, or for *not* creating pocket parks in vacant city sites, and for not redressing the glaring imbalance in the areas of public open space available to the inhabitants of rich and poor districts of the city. But it underlines the urgency of Joe Benjamin's remark about educating society to accept children on a participating basis.

With this in mind, I think there are a few exemplary enterprises around that provide glimpses of the ways in which children can be enfranchised as citizens: given challenges and responsibilities and incentives to make the city their own. I would mention, for example, the Pioneer Railway in the Buda Hills above Budapest. This is a well-known tourist attraction and the reactions of western visitors are interesting. Some see it as a carefully contrived ideological device for inculcating in the young the virtues of industrial discipline and for ensuring a supply of labour for the railway system. Others are patronising and talk of the 'comic dignity' of the 10 to 15 year old boys and girls who run it. I don't think there is anything comic about the child. The attraction for me is that the Pioneer Railway is a way of putting an essential public service into the hands of the young: of saying that they are citizens and can do something for their fellow citizens.

My other exemplary enterprises are all in this country. I am thinking of the Great George's Community Arts Project in Liverpool, and in London of Centreprise – the bookshop, coffee shop, publishing house and community resource in Hackney; Inter-Action's City Farm, and the Notting Dale Urban Studies Centre. These activities are not there for children in isolation: they aim to serve local people, young or old. They are not intended as a device for getting the kids off the street or as an antidote to vandalism. Nor are they there to entertain. They are there to help citizens, young or old, to discover their own skills, aptitudes and potentialities. They each have a focus. At the Great George's project, known locally as The Blackie (as it is housed in an old blackened former church), it is the power of the expressive arts. At Centreprise it is the power of the printed word. At the City Farm it is the power of contact with the natural world of animals and plants, and at the Notting Dale Urban Studies Centre it is the power of environmental knowledge, for children and adults alike, as a lever for change. As well as its services for local and visiting school groups it is a resource for the tenants and residents of that battered and neglected district.

I mention these examples merely to indicate that there are
people around who have accepted the message that every step
we make to take children out of the ghetto of childhood into
a sharing of interests and activities with those of the adult
world, is a step towards a more habitable environment for our
fellow citizens, young or old.

I have given emphasis to aspects of environmental learning
that happen outside school because we know, don't we, that
for many children school is, sad to say, not the place where
the vital learning experiences happen.

The Schools Council, which is the body concerned with
curriculum development in England and Wales, has
sponsored a project which I am directing at the TCPA, and
for which Eileen Adams has been seconded by the ILEA as a
Project Officer. The project is called 'Art and the Built
Environment' and is an attempt to establish a positive role in
schools and colleges of further education, for the Art
Department, not as an alternative to, or a rival to, or a
servicing agent to, the work of other departments, but as an
essential educational complement. The aims of the project are
to enlarge students' environmental perception and help them
develop a 'feel' for their urban surroundings; to enhance their
capacity for discrimination and their competence in the visual
appraisal of the built environment; and to evolve and
disseminate generally applicable techniques and methods for
achieving these objectives. We are thus involved in the
neglected field of the visual, sensory and emotional impact of
the built environment: how we *feel* about towns, what makes
us feel at home in a place and what makes us sick of the sight
of it.

We thus have a very broad approach to environmental
education, stretching from its vital compensatory function to
introduce the child to his own city, so that he or she may be
able to use it, to the neglected affective side of the child's
relationship with the environment as a task for the art teacher
– or in fact the arts teachers for language, music and drama
have surely also a part to play. Mr Russell Thompson of
Jordanhill College in Glasgow has long sought to develop an

approach to the environment through art and design.

In fact every subject in the curriculum has a part to play, once teachers are convinced of the need. I always say that this is an area of work that unites all subjects from RE to PE – and indeed there are teachers of physical education consciously involved, as I have indicated. Mr Doug McGregor when he was at Chorley College found from his enquiry the same great spread of subject teachers involved. The teacher of Modern Dance was included and when asked what was her contribution she replied that she was concerned with developing spatial awareness, and she wondered who else was. Well, of course, many geographers would claim that, in a cognitive if not in a sensory way, space and place is *their* concern. As it certainly is. Tom Masterton of Moray House in Edinburgh has developed a concentric approach to environmental studies, rural and urban for the primary teacher, taking as his text the opening recommendations in this field in the SED memorandum Primary Education. The first of these was "stress the home environment", the second was "use the home environment for the illustration of geographic phenomena" – and I would be bold enough to suggest that you can insert there any other subject-based adjective, like historic, biological or sociological. The third recommendation was "consider field work essential". In other words the study of the environment begins in the environment and not in the classroom alone.

It cannot be emphasised too strongly that the politics of the environment are not the same as they were in the '50s and '60s. Surrounded in this city, as in any British city, we are all too aware of monumental errors. Let me illustrate this with a final quotation – something which was said at a seminar I attended last year:

People have many different perspectives on their environment and on community life but only now are we beginning to see these articulated. It is not all that many years ago since people trusted local or central government to analyse their problems and prescribe the solutions. Those were the days when people accepted that new and exciting developments were bound to be better and when change seemed to be welcomed. We then moved into a period when unique prescriptive solutions gave way to the presentation of alternatives so that the public could express views before final decisions were taken. Today we face a different situation. Community groups, voluntary organisations of many kinds, and indeed individuals, now demand a say in the definition of problems and a role in determining and then implementing solutions. Even in the professional field that we normally think of as part of the establishment there are various movements concerned with re-interpreting or changing the professionals' role. Self-help groups of many kinds have sprung up, sometimes around a professional or at least advised or guided by a professional. It is quite clear that a number of people believe that the traditional professionals are not able adequately to communicate with people in a way that will help them solve their problems or make their wishes known to those who take the decisions.

Well, who said that? Actually it was Wilf Burns, the government's chief planner.

The links that geography, as a formal discipline, has with town and country planning enables it to move from the compensatory role of environmental education that I have outlined into the positive and creative role of enabling young citizens to become decision-makers on equal terms with the professionals. Public participation in planning is not just a slogan from the 1960s, it is written into our planning legislation. But it can only become a reality if we rear a generation capable of coping with the issues involved. In our slow and faltering evolution into a genuinely participatory democracy, this is the challenge to be taken up by the teacher involved in environmental education, whatever that teacher's subject may be.

5. Schooling the City Child

If I were to ask you which American thinker envisaged almost forty years ago the essential principles of an urban environmental education, it would probably take you quite a while to get round to naming the right person. The person I am thinking of was Paul Goodman, who died seven years ago. It was Goodman who, as well as anticipating the contemporary dilemmas of the urban school, and as well as showing in his well-known book *Growing Up Absurd* (a book which is now twenty years old) more clearly than any observer, how hard we have made it for the young to grow up into responsible adulthood, casually enunciated in a work of fiction the philosophy of environmental education which city teachers today are painfully evolving. How do we rear citizens who will make the city their own?

Goodman's answer was given in 1942 in his novel *The Grand Piano*, which forms part of his sprawling, shambling masterpiece *The Empire City* (now fortunately in print again as a Vintage paperback). It takes the form of a conversation between a professor of education and the hero of his novel, Horace (Horatio Alger) who is a kind of urban Huckleberry Finn, who evolves not from rags to riches like the heroes of those nineteenth-century novels by Horatio Alger Jr., but from a tarnished innocence to a battered and wise experience. Horace had the foresight to tear up his registration card on the first day of school, so that he had no official existence,

Lecture at the National Short Course on Urban Education, George Washington University, Washington DC, 10th July 1979.

except in what we have recently learned to call the informal economy, using the streets for his education ...

'On the one hand, this City is the only one you will ever have, and you must make the best of it. On the other hand, if you *want* to make the best of it, you've got to be able to criticise it and change it and circumvent it ... It seems to me *prima facie* that we have to use the City itself as our school. Instead of bringing imitation bits of the City into a school building, let us go at our own pace and get out among the real things. What I envisage is gangs of about six kids, starting at nine or ten years old, roving the City with a shepherd empowered to protect them, and accumulating experiences tempered to their powers.'

'Holy cats!' cried Horace, wide-eyed at the thought of others behaving as he did. 'They'd surely make trouble and stop the traffic!'

'So much the worse for the traffic', said the professor flatly. 'I am talking about the primary function of social life, to educate a better generation, and people tell me that the tradesmen must not be inconvenienced. I proceed. Fundamentally our kids must learn two things: Skills and Sabotage. Let me explain.

'We have here a great City and a vast culture. It must be maintained as a whole; it can and must be improved piecemeal. It is relatively permanent. At the same time it is a vast corporate organisation; its enterprise is bureaucratised, its arts are institutionalised, its mores are far from spontaneity: therefore, in order to avoid being swallowed up by it, or stamped on by it, in order to acquire and preserve a habit of freedom, a kid must learn to circumvent it and sabotage it at any needful point as occasion arises.'

'Stop! Stop' said Horace. 'Isn't this a contradiction? You say that we have to learn to be at home in the City, then you say we have to sabotage it. On the one hand we have to love and serve it; on the other hand we have to kick it. Does it make sense to you?'

'There is nothing in what you say, young man. In this City these two attitudes come to the same thing; if you persist in honest service, you will soon be engaging in sabotage. Do you follow that?'

But later Goodman reached the conclusion that "the city, under inevitable modern conditions, can no longer be dealt with practically by children" because "concealed technology, family mobility, loss of the country, loss of neighbourhood tradition and eating up of the play space have taken away the real environment".

Goodman used to describe himself as a conservative anarchist, by which he did not mean that he was an unreconstructed advocate of right-wing laissez-faire, but that he drew his sustenance from traditions which were always there.

There is a tradition in English literature, frequently met in the kind of autobiographical novel that gets adapted for television and gets exported from Britain to the United States, in the opening episodes of which our young hero (for it is seldom a heroine) is seen in the panelled classroom of the ancient small-town grammar school (and here of course in your own mythologies you substitute the little red schoolhouse) daydreaming of the woods and fields, while his elderly teacher is droning on about Latin. Once let out of school, his real life begins – wandering by the river banks and up through the woods to the hilltops, observing nature with a learning eye and absorbing the wisdom of shepherd, farmhand, forester and farrier, and from the scary old hermit whose tumbledown shack is really a treasure trove of rural lore and bygones.

In the urban equivalent, our hero is slightly lower in the social scale. Once released from his stern mentors in the grade school, he is out and down the street like a shot, everybody's friend in the street market, besieging the old lady in the candy store on the corner, begging orange boxes from the corner store, ripping off coal from the railroad yard as a rough and ready apprenticeship to the life of the city.

Years later (for such stories are invariably set in the past) these stereotypes have become successful citizens, and when they unbend to the young graduates seeking the hand of their favourite daughter, they usually confess that "I was educated in the School of Life". The point that they and their authors are making is the truism that our *real* education is gained from the physical and social environment and that 'dry-as-dust school learning', as our home-spun philosophers invariably call it, is no substitute for Life Itself.

The literary stereotypes are of course intensely literary in origin. The first owes a great deal to Wordsworth and to authors from Richard Jefferies to Laurie Lee, or in American terms from Gene Stratton Porter to Walt Disney, with the long shadow of Rousseau behind them. The second belongs to an urban picaresque tradition stretching back through Dickens to Defoe and Fielding. It too has an American tradition stretching forward from Horatio Alger Jr. to, let us say,

Herman Wouk.

Nevertheless, all the purely literary evocations of the impact of their surroundings upon the young do enshrine a truth of which every teacher must be conscious. We do know, do we not, that something has been lost, just as Paul Goodman indicated, in the incidental environmental education of both the town child and the country child, and that in any case the children we know best, whether in this country or the UK, are likely to be neither. Statistically, they are suburban children, living in an environment from which the breadwinner goes off in the morning to earn the family's livelihood in ways quite incomprehensible to the child.

This is what Goodman meant by concealed technology. The adult world of work which used to be visible, and probably all too comprehensible to the child, is no longer there. But there is another factor to add to his list of reasons why the modern city cannot be "dealt with practically by children", a factor which restricts the accessibility and usefulness of the city for old and young alike. This is the sheer opacity of the modern city.

There used to be a sense of location which every citizen would acquire quite unconsciously. It was developed to a virtuoso extent by people whose work took them to one city after another. Old-style commercial travellers in the days when they travelled by train, showbiz people doing the rounds of the theatres, antedated the Chicago school of urban geographers in knowing unerringly the structure of the traditional city. Their ankles told them the way to the riverside, their noses told them they were entering the heavy industrial sector, they instinctively empathised with the great nineteenth-century railway engineers in locating the central station.

Similarly our city fancier knew without seeing that there must be a truck-driver's snack bar round the next corner. A bibliophile knew in just what street he was likely to find a secondhand bookshop and what level of the trade he could expect to find there. A travelling salesman knew that a shop on that particular site would not pick up enough trade to be safe for credit. A lecher knew, without any red lights, that the red-light district would be over there. Hucksters, hustlers, wholesalers, junkmen and junkies, model airplane enthusiasts and people selling leotards to dancing academies, all developed a city sense which is a guide to the specialised functions of a city. Boozers knew where to find their kind of bar. Criminologists could predict the pattern of offences.

The functions and functioning of the city were transparent from its built form. But in the redeveloped city of the last three decades, our intuitions play us false. This loss of the sense of place was well described by a Scottish writer, James Finlayson, in his pamphlet, with a title that would certainly be understood in the United States, *Urban Devastation: the planning of incarceration*. One of the identifiers of a sense of location, he observed, was a hierarchy of roads and pavements, which often exists in new developments "but does not read as a hierarchy because the functions (themselves hierarchical) which it should describe are no longer visually expressed in the urban fabric. As the logic of the road and street patterns of the old cities collapses, people now need signposted directions to the community centre, to the shops, to the library, provided of course that such 'amenities' have been thought of. In old towns and cities, the environment told people where they were, the buildings 'spoke' to them and 'gave them directions'."

Well, he's right. In the rebuilt city the buildings don't talk any more, at least not in a language that makes sense to the citizen. The same kind of blandly empty or brutal facades conceal every sort of activity and every scale of activities, but they don't give any clues. In the earlier days of the modern movement in architecture people used to complain that the new school looked like a factory. But the trouble today is that so does the new city hall, the new hospital, the new apartment block and the new bus terminus. In the name of functionalism, buildings and places have ceased to proclaim their function. And the signposts don't help. They are there to guide the out-of-town motorist, not the pedestrian and certainly not for his children.

How *does* the child form his concept of the structure of the city, and in consequence develop the capacity to make the city his or her own? Anyone here searching among your early recollections will recall how your own perceptions of your physical surroundings expanded from the floor, walls and furniture of the room in the house or apartment in which you grew up, its link with other rooms, the steps, stairs, yard, garden, front door, street, shops and public park. You probably don't remember just how you put these together into some concept of the home and its relationship with the outside world, nor what gaps remained for years in your mental map of the city.

As teachers you will be familiar with the recent American work which takes our understanding beyond both Piaget's work and the original studies by Kevin Lynch: the work of people like Robert Maurer and James Baxter, Roger Hart, Gary Moore and David Stea. They point out that Lynch's *The Image of the City*, while drawing upon what Kenneth Boulding calls the "spatial image" and the "relational image", ignores those components of our picture of the city which he calls the "value image" and the "emotional image". The aspects of the environment which are most attractive for some children may very well be the ones from which the adult world averts its eyes. I was told, for example, that here in Washington at the symposium on 'Children, Nature and the Urban Environment' my friend Simon Nicholson persuaded fifth-graders from the Stevens Elementary School to write about 'Our city and the places where we play'. The children insisted on describing the derelict Scarey Dairy where rats and broken glass were two of the attractions. The School Board, in whose perception the Scarey Dairy just doesn't exist, was unnecessarily embarrassed.

It is part of the orthodoxy of child development that girls are abler than boys of the same age in verbal ability, while boys' spatial ability is far greater than that of girls. The work of the cognitive mappers is cited to confirm this. John Brierley (one of the English inspectors of schools for the Department of Education) reporting on tests which involve proficiency in the manipulation of spatial relationships indicating the greater ability of boys even from the age of two, argues that it is very likely that visuo-spatial proficiency is under the control of the sex chromosome-hormone machinery and has its roots in the right hemisphere development of the brain. His conclusion is that "for practical purposes at school these findings strengthen the importance of systematic exposure of girls to early experience with toys, sand, water and boxes, which introduce numerical and spatial relationships, for by doing so might we improve mathematical ability later on".

Is the environment of the urban child better or worse than it used to be? From our own recollections or from the opening pages of innumerable autobiographies we may be likely to conclude that the contemporary child has a less happy habitat than that of his grandparents. Then we reflect that the distorting mirror of memory and the transforming power of nostalgia may be playing its usual tricks. For the social historians are at our elbows to remind us, as Peter Laslett does, that "Englishmen in 1901 had to face the disconcerting fact that destitution was still an outstanding feature of fully industrialised society, with a working class perpetually liable to social and material degradation. More than half of all the children of working men were in this dreadful condition, which meant forty per cent of all the children in the country. These were the scrawny, dirty, hungry, ragged, verminous boys and girls who were to grow up into the working class of twentieth-century England."

The modern city child survives, while his predecessor a century ago frequently did not. But once we go beyond the giant steps to survival owed to sanitation, water supply, preventative medicine and social security, and attempt to look qualitatively at the lives the modern city offers to its children, doubts and worries emerge. We begin to think that there *is* a difference between the slums of hope and the slums of despair, and between being poor and being part of a culture of poverty.

The concept of a culture of poverty, like that of the cycle of deprivation, has given rise to passionate ideological argument. Oscar Lewis, the American anthropologist who invented the phrase, simply remarked that in Cuba, or in the squatter cities of Peru, Turkey, Athens, Hong Kong and Brazil, there are millions of poor people but little sign of a culture of poverty; and a related point, specifically to do with the environment of the urban child, emerged from the international survey directed for UNESCO by Kevin Lynch. This was concerned with children of eleven to fourteen years in the city of Salta in Argentina; in the western suburbs of Melbourne, Australia; in Toluca, a provincial capital in Mexico, and in Ecatepec, a largely dweller-built settlement on the northern fringe of Mexico City; in two contrasted neighbourhoods in Warsaw, and two similarly contrasted neighbourhoods of another Polish city, Cracow.

The UNESCO survey was probably the most ambitious attempt yet made to evaluate the relationship between children and the urban environment. The techniques used were those of 'cognitive mapping' and interviews. What emerges very clearly is that these older children's picture of the city and their part in it is conditioned by the esteem in which it is held by their elders. The Melbourne children, for example, were certainly the most affluent in this international sample. They were "tall, well dressed, almost mature, apparently full of vitality" but they see themselves as the bottom of society, and "if these Australians have hopes for themselves or their children, it is to be somebody else, and to get away". The Argentine children, on the other hand, are quite obviously conscious of being members of a community with "features which make it amenable to change at their scale of possibility". Only three of the interviewed children there thought they would leave the area in the future, while only three of the Melbourne children thought they would stay.

Alone in the UNESCO survey, the children of Ecatepec, the dweller-built settlement outside Mexico City, "consistently named their school as a favourite place, and gave it a loving emphasis on their maps". The suggestions they made to the interviewers "reflect a genuine concern for their families, as well as their own future, and an empathy for fellow residents of the *colonia*". They were the poorest children in the survey, and to the adult researchers their environment was harsh, bleak and monotonous, and it is obvious from their report that they were puzzled by the unique affection for their school displayed in the maps, drawings and interviews of the children of Ecatepec. "This must be a tribute to the public education in that place", they surmise. No such tribute would be offered by the children of an equivalently poor district in Detroit, Boston, London or Liverpool, though it might have been made there many years ago.

The parents of those Mexican children are poor rural migrants who made the great leap from rural hopelessness into the inner city slums of Mexico City. Once they has learned urban ways, they moved to a squatter settlement on the fringe of the city. In many such Latin American settlements the parents have built their own schools and hired their own teachers. For their children life is visibly improving, "there is less dust now, houses that used to be shanties are fully constructed, one does not have to go outside the *colonia* for certain services ..." The parents from Melbourne, with an infinitely higher standard of living, are conscious that they haven't quite made it, and the stigmatisation of the district where they live communicates itself to the children. In this place where "football clubs and schools have two-metre high wire mesh fence around the periphery topped with barbed wire" and where parks are "flat featureless tracts of haphazardly grassed unused land", the local authorities believe that "space for organised team sport is what is most urgently needed, despite the lack of use of what already exists".

It is hard, no doubt, for those who have devoted themselves to campaigning for physical space for the young in the city, a claim which is certainly self-justifying, to accustom themselves to the idea that very early in life another just as urgent and more difficultly-met demand arises, for *social* space: the claim of the city's children to be part of the city's life.

Kevin Lynch's own conclusion from his international survey was that the young people interviewed were victims of "experiential starvation". He found that distance is not the essential restriction on the movement of young adolescents away from their local areas. More important is the mixture of parental control, personal fear and a lack of knowledge of how to get about, as well as the availability and cost of public transport. There are many other ways in which the contemporary urban environment is less usable, less

comprehensible and less equipped with opportunities for
growth into adulthood than the traditional city. Domination
of the physical environment by the needs of the driver of the
out-of-town motor vehicle is one example of this. Just try
crossing a city like Birmingham on foot. The change in retail
distribution from corner shop to supermarket, and the change
in the pattern of housing from the street with front doors and
back yards to the super-block are further examples of the way
in which it is harder for the child to cope with his environment,
let alone use it for his own purposes. It is not at all surprising
that so many adolescents seem to be actively at war with their
environment.

The boy or girl in the familiar background of poverty and
deprivation is more and more isolated from the world of the
successful and self-confident as time goes by.

Inner city teachers, even very experienced ones, are so
accustomed to mobility, freedom of access to transport and
social competence in getting around that they are continually
surprised that so many of the children they teach lead lives
confined to a few streets, or blocks. Very significantly,
although this point is seldom made in the literature of urban
education, it is very frequently made in the literature of
juvenile delinquency. Innumerable studies of delinquent
children in the world's cities stress their isolation. Aryeh
Leissner, with experience of both New York and Tel Aviv,
remarks that "street club workers were constantly aware of the
feelings of isolation which pervaded the atmosphere". In
Chicago, J.F. Short and F.L. Strodbeck noted that "the range
of gang boys' physical movements is severely restricted" not
just for fear of other gangs, but also because of a "more general
lack of social assurance". James Patrick found the same "social
disability" in the Glasgow boys he observed. This lack of social
assurance certainly does amount to a social disability for many
city children. Some children steal, not because they have no
access to the purchase money, but because they find it a less
arduous transaction than the verbal encounter with the seller.
They move like strangers through their own city.

All our generalisation about the city child are about the poor
or deprived child. The child from a better-off family, or simply

from one more equipped with urban know-how, is far better
able to exploit the wonderful potential that any city offers. He
has learned how to use its facilities. Blessed is the child, rich
or poor, with a hobby or a skill or an all-consuming passion,
for he or she is motivated to utilise the city as a generator of
happiness. There are plenty of juvenile passions, of course,
which are generators of misery for other people, but it remains
true that the child who is hooked on to some network built
around a shared activity has found ways of making the city
work for him. An enormous range of possible experiences and
activities are open to the city child, and as always the
household which is accustomed to planning ahead and knows
where to look things up draws the maximum benefit from
opportunities which are theoretically available to all the city's
children. The leader of the Inner London Education
Authority remarked to me sadly that "What ever new facility
we provide, we know in advance that it's the middle class
children who will draw the benefit". Significantly it is the
quality newspapers and not the popular ones which find it
worthwhile to include features on holiday events and activities
for children. In my own city those children who are endowed
with what middle class sociologists sneer at as 'middle class
values' are set upon an escalator of experiences and activities
which they travel up, at the public expense, so that the gap
continually widens in the degree of urban competence and
control over their own destinies which they enjoy, compared
with that of the children who never set foot on this escalator.

The isolated child in the city is unfamiliar with the public
transport system, with the use of the telephone, with the public
library service, with eliciting information from strangers, with
the norms of behaviour in cafés and restaurants, with planning
his activities in advance, with articulating or responding to
requests from outside the immediate family circle. The reader
might well wonder as to whether such a child really exists, and
the answer is that children as isolated as this from the
mainstream of urban life exist in very large numbers. I have
mentioned the existence of such ideas as the 'culture of
poverty' or of 'cycles of deprivation', each of which has its
passionate opponents who see them as modern versions of the

Victorian equation of poverty with sin, the idea that the poverty of the poor is their own fault, or as an assumption of the superiority of middle class values.

But if we simply want to know why so large a proportion of inner city children grow up unable to manipulate their environment in the way that is taken for granted in the middle class home, we are bound to look for explanations in the social isolation of the home of the modern inner city child, soberly analysed by Martin Deutsch in these terms: "Visually, the urban slum and its overcrowded apartments offer the child a minimal range of stimuli. There are usually few if any pictures on the wall, and the objects of the household, be they toys, furniture or utensils, tend to be sparse, repetitious and lacking in form and colour variations. The sparsity of objects and lack of diversity of home artefacts which are available and meaningful to the child, in addition to the unavailability of individualised training, gives the child few opportunities to manipulate and organise the visual properties of his environment and thus perceptually to organise and discriminate the nuances of that environment ... It is true, as has been pointed out frequently, that the pioneer child didn't have many playthings either. But he had a more active responsibility towards the environment and a great variety of growing plants and other natural resources as well as a stable family that assumed a primary role for the education and training of the child."

The tragedy of the isolated child and the dilemma of all our efforts to alleviate his deprivation were poignantly expressed by John and Elizabeth Newson as they reached the third stage of their long-term study of child-rearing in an English city. They remarked that they are continually asked to specify how children should be brought up, while they have never claimed to be capable of giving such advice. They have, however, reached a conclusion: "Parents at the upper end of the social scale are more inclined *on principle* to use democratically based, highly verbal means of control, and this kind of discipline is likely to produce personalities who can both identify successfully with the system and use it to their own ends later on. At the bottom of the scale, in the unskilled group, parents choose *on principle* to use a highly authoritarian, mainly non-verbal means of control, in which words are used more to threaten and bamboozle the child into obedience than to make him understand the rationale behind social behaviour: and this seems likely to result in a personality who can neither identify with nor beat the system. In short, privileged parents, by using the methods they prefer, produce children who expect as of right to be privileged and who are very well equipped to realise these expectations; while deprived parents, *also by using the methods they prefer*, will probably produce children who expect nothing and are not equipped to do anything about it. Thus the child born into the lowest social bracket has everything stacked against him *including his parents' principles of child upbringing*."

This is a bleak conclusion, made all the more pointed by the fact that it is the outcome of many years of investigation and reflection. It underlines the vital compensatory role of nursery education, of efforts to improve the quality of child-minding, and of all those attempts in and out of schools to enlarge the environmental experience and capability of inner city children.

And for this, to return to the ancient wisdom of Paul Goodman, with which I began, "the streets and working places of the city must be made safer and more available. The idea of city planning is for children to be able to *use* the city, for no city is governable if it does not grow citizens who feel it is theirs."

6. *Where do we go from here?*

Since our project has been concerned with our sensory, emotional and affective relationship with the buildings of our daily environment, let me confess that the RCA is full of happy associations for me. And, as usual, it isn't just a matter of architecture, though I do think that this is one of the more successful of London's post-war buildings. Indeed without disrespect for the architects, Casson and Cadbury-Brown, one of my favourite structures in this particular institution is the group of hundred-year-old corrugated iron sheds down the road, housing the sculpture school. They constitute one of the oldest temporary and prefabricated buildings in London and sooner or later are certain to be listed as being of architectural or historic interest. This is one of the perils of that latitudinarian approach to architecture that people like me are guilty of advocating.

Another of my happy associations is with this very hall we are in now. Here I saw a performance of Mozart's *Zaide* put on by students from this college and from the Royal College of Music over the road. Musically, it was just a kind of pre-echo of his fully-finished later operas, but it was done with such style, such wit and enthusiasm that it reminded me of what I regard as one of the great moral fables of curriculum innovation.

I will come to that in a minute. I need to mention a further association that the Royal College of Art has for me. I associate

Address to the concluding Summer School of the Schools Council 'Art and the Built Environment' project, Royal College of Art, London, 17th July 1982.

it with William Richard Lethaby, one of my mentors from the past. He died, as it happens, 51 years ago this very day, so I only know him through his reputation and his writings. In the 1890s, when the London County Council was in one of its leftward lurches, like the GLC today, he was art adviser to the LCC's Technical Education Board, and complained that the curriculum of the average art school made him think of learning to swim in a thousand lessons without water. This is, of course, precisely the same complaint that we make today about environmental education. You cannot be expected to learn or teach about the environment without enabling the student to experience it directly.

The LCC appointed Lethaby as the first principal of its Central School of Arts and Crafts and he made the place the best school in Europe at a time when the Royal College of Art was, as he put it, "the worst school in Europe". Inevitably he was called upon to work his magic here too and was appointed the first professor of design here. Lethaby was famous for his aphoristic wit and his friends used to note down his odd sayings. He used to remark that "education is better underdone than overdone. It must look beyond the barrier of books". (Rather a chastening thought for people like me today, busy promoting the book of the project.) He would explain that he was a socialist because he believed that "to live on the labour of others is a form of cannibalism".

Lethaby used to say that "little can be proved: what matters is the quality of our assumptions". His own assumptions were few and simple. He assumed that the most important thing in education, as in life, was art and that "the helplessness of modern art is the measure of the helplessness of the workers: there is justice in the universe". Lethaby declared that "those who believe in the condensed ignorance called Higher Education have succeeded with great difficulty in at last creating a dislike for that greatest of blessings, work".

Our situation today is of course worse than Lethaby imagined. We have to come to terms with the implications for schools of those well-known lines from the American folk song 'Halleluyah, I'm a Bum': "Oh why don't you work, like the other guys do? / How the hell can I work when there's no work to do?" But Lethaby did have a remark to offer us in our present dilemmas. In 1916, in the middle of the First World War, he gave a lecture on 'Town Tidying', which has stayed with me ever since I first read it in the middle of the Second World War. It is quoted in at least three of my books, whatever I was writing about.

Lethaby said: "For the earliest part of my life I was quieted by being told that ours was the richest country in the world, until I woke up to know that what I meant by riches was learning and beauty, and music and art, coffee and omelettes; perhaps in the coming days of poverty we may get more of these."

I know this sentence by heart and I repeat it to myself whenever I hear any politician, of right or left, talking about education.

The cry has been going up for years, 'back to basics', implying that the education system has been concentrating on inessentials and that the collapse of British manufacturing industry is a result of this educational sabotage. This onslaught started long before the present government. If Sir Keith Joseph and Dr Rhodes Boyson resigned tomorrow, or if the government resigned tomorrow, nothing at all would change except that we would all have a different team of Aunt Sallies to hate.

I agree with the remark of Michael Storm, the ILEA environmental studies advisor, in the current *Bulletin of Environmental Education*, where he suggests that "perhaps we should seek to replace the dreary slogan 'Back to Basics' with our own version, 'Out to Basics'." Basic things, for me, are Lethaby's learning and beauty, and music and art, coffee and omelettes.

Michael Storm was explaining his view that:

We will most easily rebut any charges of parochialism if environmental work is seen as a dimension of the whole curriculum, not as a separate compartment. Sometimes, the very elaborate claims made for local study are unhelpful, I think. Colleagues may say: 'Why do you want to take pupils out (thereby disrupting institutional arrangements)? This neighbourhood is already too familiar to them; they know more about it than you do.' And so on. To counter these reservations, we should probably make much more use of the 'communication skills' rationale for environmental work. Local study which establishes *no* new knowledge about an area is of course justifiable as pupils discover new ways of classifying, recording, presenting, selecting. Environmental work, by providing experiences that pupils *want* to talk, act, draw and write about, regularly enhances the effectiveness of the wider curriculum.

He wasn't talking about subject boundaries, he was talking about education and he was urging us to claim that the kind of work displayed all around you in the exhibitions accompanying this conference is central, not marginal, to the process of education.

I now come to my operatic fable which was brought to my mind by the performance of *Zaide* I attended in this hall. You will hardly believe me but, sixty years ago, Mozart's *Magic Flute* was not a very well-known opera in this country. If it was performed, it was done before the First World War in a curiously garbled version of its set-piece arias under the name *Il Flauto Magico*, as though it was an Italian opera, not a Viennese pantomime. In 1919 a music teacher called Charles Smith staged a performance of the *Magic Flute* with boys aged seven to thirteen in an elementary school on the Isle of Dogs, then as now a run-down corner of the East End of London. The late professor Edward Dent found it "astonishingly convincing" and a distinguished singer who went with him to see it said to him "I have sung in this opera dozens of times in Germany; I now understand it for the first time".

People said to him: "You must have a marvellous bunch of kids down there. Maybe it's all that fresh air blowing across the docks." So he went to another LCC elementary school in Whitechapel and coaxed another performance out of the children there.

Nobody expected Mr Smith to do the *Magic Flute*. The education authority and the Board of Education didn't ask him to get involved in curriculum innovation. He had a class set of fifty copies of the *National Song Book* in tonic sol-fa. Why didn't he settle down to 'Strawberry Fair', 'Oh, No John' and 'Hearts of Oak' like any other sensible teacher? There wasn't even a Schools Council project on hand to accuse him of cultural élitism and hand him out a few tin whistles to rescue the neglected indigenous culture of the Isle of Dogs.

Now times really have changed since then. During the course of our project, children from one of our London comprehensives took part in the making of a best-selling record, not of the *Magic Flute* but of a song with the refrain they sang:

> *We don't need no education*
> *We don't need no thought control*
> *No dark sarcasm in the classroom.*
> *Teacher, leave us kids alone.* *

as though school was a species of child-molesting.

That song promoted an image of school as a place where obedience and subservience to a ruling class ideology, with flag-waving nationalism, religious superstition and royalty-worship are inculcated. Maybe this picture of school was true in the days when Mr Smith was doing the *Magic Flute*, but it is quite preposterous nowadays.

These characteristics are certainly at large in society today. They are promoted by the media, by our unbelievable popular press, by our cynically manipulated commercial entertainments industry. But not by school. Not by teachers.

I am much more worried about the profoundly anti-educational atmosphere that surrounds the young than I am by cuts in the expansion of educational spending. Part of the reason for this is that in the boom decades after the war, education and the rewards it brings were oversold. Every additional bit of expenditure, every increase in student numbers at the upper and more expensive end of the system, every new development in educational technology, was a step towards some great social goal and would yield rewards all round. But it has not delivered the goods.

In the raw material commodity markets of the world, people trade in what are called futures: wheat, cotton or coffee not yet harvested, minerals not yet extracted. Sometimes

---

* The lyric is from Pink Floyd's 1979 album *Another Brick in the Wall*. I should add that in the discussion following this lecture some continental teachers said that my comments on this performance were missing the point. They said that in, for example, the Netherlands, school students saw this song as a kind of anthem expressing their perception of the school system.

speculators oversell these futures. The education industry has sold too many futures to too many people. The small investors feel that they have been taken for a ride. They want their money back.

When the bottom fell out of the world sisal market, Julius Nyerere asked: "What are we to do with our sisal? We can't eat it?" And you can't eat art. It is a self-justifying activity that has been going on ever since cavemen painted their caves, but it doesn't do much for the balance of payments. (But, in my view, the idea that schools are responsible for the decline of manufacturing industry is hypocritical nonsense: if we were really concerned with promoting growth industries we would be preparing children for careers in insurance broking and tourism. Or we would be honest enough to suggest that they could make themselves a happy and varied working life in the so-called informal economy, outside the official employment spectrum altogether.)

But every contracting industry has its casualties. The Art and the Built Environment Project began its life not in an academic institution but in the education unit of a poverty-stricken voluntary organisation, the Town and Country Planning Association. This very month, the TCPA has felt obliged to cut the umbilical cord of its education unit and its journal, the *Bulletin of Environmental Education*, *BEE*, who are starting a new life on their own as *Streetwork*. I hope that teachers who have valued *BEE* will continue to support it.

The Schools Council itself has received its death sentence.

Well, so what? you might ask, and I too have been one of its innumerable critics. So also have been many of its own temporary and permanent employees. Well over a decade ago, several of the people – like Geoff Cooksey and Tony Light – who flitted through the unenviable role of joint secretary, were urging that curriculum development began and ended inside the school or never got off the ground. We, and the project, have had nothing but continual help and encouragement from the curriculum officer Maurice Plaskow and from the Art Committee chairman Ernest Goodman, the former head of Manchester High School of Art: that marvellous anachronism which, while he was still there, was a permanent reproach to the whole trend in the organisation of art education in the '50s and '60s to upgrade the institutions to higher education status. An ordinary secondary school built around an art-based curriculum: what a marvellous dream it seems – and how it was betrayed by élitism and the status-race!

This meeting may be an incidental wake for the Schools Council itself, just as it marks the conclusion of our own project, a very minor one in terms of Schools Council investment but it also represents a triumph for both, if I may say so. What the Schools Council did was to buy a little *time* for an essentially time-consuming activity – the dissemination of ideas and methods which were there already, in and out of school, among wider circles of teachers. As with other projects in other subjects, the guarantee of effectiveness was the existence of networks of teachers in different areas which had already overcome the isolation of the individual department in individual schools. Those local education authorities who employ art advisers have been valuable to the project in providing a ready-made link between schools and between art teachers.

Her Majesty's Inspectorate are a body of people which shows no sign of being axed as a superfluous quango, and its members often remind us that they are older than the local authority education system, they were there before the Board of Education, the Ministry of Education or the Department of Education and Science. Sometimes I wonder what they do with their independence. But our project owes its inception to HMI Ralph Jeffery who quietly steered it through innumerable thickets in the jungle of educational bureaucracy and it has an enormous debt to the late HMI Daniel Shannon, who pioneered the links between teachers in schools and architects and planners outside them. This link, which seems so simple and desirable, often happens at a personal level, but Dan Shannon, particularly in the series of teachers' courses he instigated at Cheltenham, Bath and Leeds, tried to make it a habit.

So where do we go from here? In general educational terms, I can only repeat the words I used at the very beginning of this particular adventure: "When we consider how little the massive educational spending of the last decade did to enhance the lives or life-chances of the children in what is known as 'the lower quartile of the ability range' in secondary education we may perhaps hope that the new age of frugality will lead us to devise appropriate educational experiences in a climate where we make fewer grandiose claims for what the school can do. By settling for less, we might even achieve more."

Five years later, I have no reason to change my opinion. Curriculum development depends on teachers. If they think that art is a marginal aspect of what happens in schools, that is inevitably what it will be.

When I speak of art I mean, of course, all the arts and I urge the kind of collaboration which can never be stimulated from outside the school, between teachers in arts subjects and geographers, historians and biologists, in environmental work. How absurd to imagine that approaches to the environment through different traditions and disciplines are mutually exclusive, when we all know in our experience as individuals that they are mutually complementary as well as mutually necessary.

Circumstances differ enormously from school to school, as anyone who has had the privilege of visiting vast numbers of schools will attest. But anyone with faith in the importance of his or her particular contribution can, without waiting for an officially-stamped passport, become, like Mr Smith blowing his Magic Flute in the Isle of Dogs, the pied pipers of educational innovation. But a little encouragement does help!

7. Places for Learning

All places are learning places. From infancy children have learned from their surroundings, watching parents and neighbours, learning how they set about their work and copying them. But as work moved out of the home and into the factory, so the unconscious learning of the home environment was replaced by deliberate teaching in special places called schools. Manual skills in manipulating materials, like the arts of the potter, the carpenter, the farmer or the cook, were seen as something separate from intellectual skills like reading and calculating. In Western societies schools have existed all through history, simply as places where a small minority of boys were trained to be priests or scribes, learning the mysteries of religion or literacy. The idea that everyone should be enabled to learn everything belongs to the modern world. In not much more than a century schools have grown from simple classrooms to complex institutions. Higher education has similarly evolved from Socrates discoursing with his pupils in an Athenian square to the modern university full of specialist places like lecture theatres and laboratories. This paper is about the physical surroundings of education. What do learning places teach us?

Learning before schooling

We have all been children, and even if we have forgotten, our parents always remember the day we first crawled across the room, the day we walked unaided, our own exploration of gardens, woods and fields, or our first sight of the sea. But

Lecture at the Department of Architecture, Massachusetts Institute of Technology, Cambridge, Massachusetts, November 1987. Another version was published in *Lifestyles* (edited by Peter Marsh), Oxford: Andromeda, 1991.

children themselves often remember best small physical details and sensations: the coldness of metal, the mystery of glass, the feel of the surface of the stairs we laboriously climbed up and down, the texture of wool or silk, the fur of an animal.

The child's world expands to the street and its shops and services, new sights, sounds and smells. Whether it is in city, suburb or village, it is a vivid sensory experience, a learning situation. Obviously the younger children are, the closer are their eyes to the ground, and this is one of the reasons why the *floorscape* – the texture and subdivisions of flooring and paving, as well as changes of level in steps and slopes (small enough to walk up for an adult, big enough to sit on for a child) – is very much more significant for the young. When urban geographers in the United States asked adults what they remembered from their early childhood, they named particularly the floor of their environment, the tactile rather than the visual qualities of their surroundings.

Very soon the child is avidly observing objects in the street, naming vehicles, noticing the garbage truck, the ambulance, the fire engine, and naming the letters on street signs, shops and stores, endlessly asking their meaning and eager to learn.

By this time the fortunate child is already attending a day nursery or a playgroup, interacting with other children and manipulating a new environment. For many today this is the first chance they have to experiment with the materials of building: bricks, wood, water and sand. Not many such groups are organised in specially-built premises. Most are run, often by parents themselves, in private houses, church halls or in schools with a room to spare. Apart from strong tables and chairs of the right size, the essentials are the things themselves and the space to use them, including outside areas for games, for digging and using cycles, scooters and push-along toys.

This kind of learning came naturally and inevitably in the simpler societies when the child was, and in many parts of the world still is, part of the family as an economic unit. In modern sophisticated societies the opportunities have to be provided deliberately. Research in Britain and the United States shows that the advantage of this early learning are still evident several years later.

But the environment does not cease to be a place for learning simply because after a certain age children are obliged to spend a certain part of their time contained in schools. Most of their daylight hours are not in school.

In their infant years most children everywhere look forward to school, even though sometimes with anxiety. In their teens most children in the rich world yearn to get out of school. They want to be *streetwise*. In the poor world, where children gain their street wisdom at an early age, children value schooling. For them it ends all too soon. They yearn for the chances that the rich world takes for granted.

Beginning school

In the centuries when schools were places where boys were prepared to be clerks or clerics, the environment of schooling was simple. A classical education required books and writing materials, a teacher and a class. Nothing more. It could be conducted in a private house, a church or any available room. When places were specially built to serve as schools, they were bleak and bare. No concessions were made to the nature of childhood, nor even to the comfort of pupils. Our mental image is of ancient buildings with rows of dusty benches in which generations of boys had carved their initials, of dreary mechanical learning and of stern punishments.

This impression is as old as schooling itself. Shakespeare wrote of "the whining schoolboy, with his satchel, and shining morning face, creeping like snail unwillingly to school", and the poet William Wordsworth regretted in some famous lines that "shades of the prison-house begin to close upon the growing boy".

Two hundred years ago a handful of pioneers began a slow revolution in education which laid the foundations of what we would now call *child-centred* education. The most famous were Jean-Jacques Rousseau (1712-1778), Johann Heinrich Pestalozzi (1746-1827) and Friedrich Froebel (1782-1852). Endless educational experiments in Europe and America can be traced back to the ideas they set in motion . Their revolution took several forms.

The first was the idea that schooling was for girls as well as boys. Until this was accepted rich girls had governesses and poor girls learned from their mothers or taught themselves. The second was the idea that *every* child was entitled to an education, whether or not parents could afford to do without its labour or earnings. The third was a result of this, the idea that schooling should be free, universal and compulsory. The fourth was the idea of infant education: schooling should begin in early childhood. The fifth was the idea that education ought to extend beyond reading, writing, religion and arithmetic. It should include the sciences, arts and manual skills.

All these ideas had been tried long before in particular places. Individual teachers in European cities or in the little red schoolhouse of New England townships pioneered every widening of education. This tells us that the teacher is more important than the classroom, certainly more important than the institution. Think back to your own schooldays and of the particular teacher who actually influenced you.

None of these pioneers thought it necessary to make recommendations about the *design* of schools. Rousseau's *Emile*, the child who gives his name to his treatise on education, has a one-to-one relationship with his tutor with the freedom of a country house, its farms and woods. Emile's school is the whole rural environment. Pestalozzi read Rousseau's book, abandoned his career and became a farmer. He began a school for destitute children, intended that they should work in the fields in the summer and weave and spin in the winter, picking up a basic education when not working. Froebel had been inspired by Pestalozzi and set up his own school in a peasant's cottage. Later he became interested in pre-school education and in 1840 he started the first kindergarten.

All modern ideas about play and its place in education can be traced back to him. He developed a series of Gifts, Occupations, Games and Songs which he thought appropriate to different stages of a child's growth. The 'Gifts' began with a woollen ball, to be given to a child at three months. The next was a wooden sphere, a cube and a cylinder, followed by a series of subdivisions of the cube. Further gifts, wooden rings and sticks followed. America's most celebrated twentieth century architect, Frank Lloyd Wright, was reared on Froebel's Gifts by his Froebel-trained mother. Architectural historians trace their influence on his early work.

Jug, clay or flower?

The idea of child-centred education and the encouragement of the child in exploration of its world and experimentation with the physical environment were the most significant of the changes that slowly crept into our ideas about schooling. If you strip away the language of theory you find that there are three attitudes to childhood:

- The child is an empty jug to be filled. This is the traditional view. There is a body of learning and basic skills of language and number that has to be poured into the jug. These are called subjects, and the school curriculum in the twentieth century has broadened to include an ever-widening range of human knowledge. When a new public issue arises, like road safety, sexual hygiene or computer literacy, it is the task of the school to pour this too into the jug. The jug theory implies that the children are lined up in rows to receive this wisdom. This is the traditional classroom design.

- The child is a lump of clay to be moulded by a skilled potter, the teacher. Society wants good citizens, so the child must be shaped into citizenship. Religions want believers, so the child must be formed by religious belief. Employers need workers, so the child must be disciplined into reliable working habits. This model too implies the classroom deliberately isolated from outside influences which might impede the potter's work.

- The child is a flower to be lovingly nurtured, given the right growing conditions and allowed to develop in its own way. This is the child-centred approach and it implies that the school environment should be designed for the needs of the child. There should be child-sized furniture, a welcoming colour scheme, small groups instead of rows of desks. The teacher is a helper and stimulator, not a formidable instructor.

Our problem is that we tend to hold all three of these attitudes at the same time. We want the child to be jug, clay and flower, all three, and when children fail to live up to this expectation we blame the child, or the school, or ourselves. Usually the school.

Ideas about school design have continually changed in the last hundred years. Any old person attending a concert or drama in a modern junior school always remarks that 'schools weren't like this when I was young!' They remember high railings around the schoolyard and notice boards with the message 'Parents Are Not Allowed Beyond This Point'. They remember that window sills used to be high enough to prevent children from looking out, and they notice today that they are low enough to ensure that the children can. They remember the rows of benches and desks all facing the teacher, and they see that today children are often working in small groups around individual tables with the teacher circulating among them. If they were reared in the country in a one-room school where all ages of children were taught together, they are surprised by the number of specialist rooms in the modern school for arts, crafts, sciences and language teaching. School architects like to think that the school is a learning laboratory. A regrettable number of children see it as a prison.

Most of all, the old are surprised by the size and scale of contemporary secondary education. It is often a surprise to the young too. The head of a village school asked "Can you imagine what it means for a child to go from my school, with 31 pupils, to the secondary school miles away, which has 2,750?" The size of schools is a hotly-contended area of educational politics. Parents favour small schools in both primary and secondary education. They see the small school as a more intimate, friendly institution to which both they and their children can relate. Administrators favour the large school claiming both the economies of scale that apply in other industries and the possibility of a wider range of subject expertise. Small size is seen as an advantage in the private sector of education and as an anachronism in the public sector. It is only publicly-funded schools that are closed because of their small size.

Research into the relationship between school size and educational performance is hard to conduct, partly because we are not all agreed on what we expect of schools, and partly because of differences in the social class and home background of pupils. One of the most significant of all pieces of experimental research on the effect of size of schools on children was carried out in the United States and replicated in Canada, and on a smaller scale in Cheshire, England. It found that "students from the large schools *were exposed* to a larger number of school activities and the best of them achieved standards in many activities that were unequalled by students in small schools; on the other hand, students in the small schools *participated* in more activities – academic, inter-school, cultural and extracurricular; their versatility and performance scores were consistently higher, they reported more and 'better' satisfactions, and displayed stronger motivation in all areas of school activity".

This carefully-worded summary of research findings is the closest we can get at present to an answer to our questions on the effect of school buildings in terms of size on children. But there are other aspects of learning places. In the kindergarten and the infant school we take it for granted that the atmosphere should be as home-like as possible but that at the same time it should be a workshop for children to explore their world. Once children are in their teens the school becomes a workshop for formal learning. It is also a workshop for their teachers who need an environment for effective performance of *their* skills.

The almighty wall

The school is the daily environment of children for a few vital years whose effects last for a lifetime. It is also the environment of teachers for their working lifetime. Well over a century ago a famous Victorian headteacher, Edward Thring of Uppingham, made a startling remark about this:

Whatever men may say or think, the Almighty Wall is, after all, the supreme and final arbiter of schools. I mean no living power in the world can overcome the dead, unfeeling, everlasting pressure of the permanent structures, of the permanent conditions under which work has to be done. Never rest till you have got all the fixed machinery for work, the best possible. The waste in a teacher's workshop is the lives of men.

He ignored the fact that in his day as well as ours a majority of teachers were women. But he was making a point that is endlessly ignored. Most people at work, even in the most computerised office environment or factory work-station on an assembly line, instinctively personalise their workspace. Railwaymen have their own shacks by the trackside, truck drivers decorate their cabs. Teachers too like to stamp their style on their surroundings, if only in filling a cupboard with the books that are important to them and to have the materials they use around them.

In any system of compulsory education the teacher is both professionally and legally in charge of the class. The 'almighty wall' is the classroom wall and it needs to serve the needs of that group of pupils and that particular teacher during that lesson. Schools and colleges in different countries and with different ages of children operate in a variety of ways. School architects have debated for years on the different virtues of a horizontal (long corridors) or a vertical (frequent staircases) design of school, a matter which is frequently settled for them by the available site. Education planners similarly debate over horizontal (related to a year-group) or a vertical (related to proficiency in a particular subject) design of the timetable.

But movement around the school building, or complex of buildings, is the first thing any visitor notices. Schools and colleges in different countries and with different ages of children operate in a variety of ways. Sometimes the pupils move to the home-bases of particular teachers, sometimes the teachers move with their personal equipment from room to room. Sometimes the rooms themselves (workshops, art rooms, laboratories, gymnasia) are equipped with the equipment for a specialist field of learning or activity.

Other teachers have simply a body of knowledge and a love of their particular subject to impart. They carry their teaching aids around with them. But language teachers, for example, like to surround the room with posters, printed matter and objects which evoke the culture of another country, just to bring to the notice of their pupils that real people speak that language in a real context and that it is worth knowing. The happiest teachers are often those in art and craft subjects, whose workshop is filled with things that provide a justification

for the skills they try to pass on. Often theirs are the happiest
classes too. They are the least popular with the caretaker or
janitor because they generate the most mess and untidiness.
But they are the teachers who have the Almighty Wall on their
side.

Open planning

By the 1960s and 1970s in several countries there was a trend
to push down the walls. Just as we saw the growth of open-plan
or 'landscaped' offices, so we had open-plan primary schools.
The arguments were the same. Corridors are waste space, usable
for nothing except getting around. Cut them out and have a
free-flowing environment for all. It happens on the factory
floor, why not everywhere else? It is also cheaper to build.

In offices it was made possible by two things: universal
carpeting and the fact that modern business machines are
quiet. Why not apply the same approach to schools? The idea
is to give each teacher and class a 'home base' separated only
by furniture and cupboards from a series of 'activity areas'
through which the children flow from one lesson to another.

Does it work? Do children and teachers like it? This is a question
answered in different ways by different researchers. Perhaps,
just as in offices, it depends upon each individual's personal
psychology. Perhaps extroverts enjoy continual interaction with
others. Perhaps introverts prefer and need a secure enclosed nest.

One group of British researchers into open-plan infant
schools (age five to seven) found that teachers there spent less
time actually talking to pupils and more time on the routine
of school management. They also found that children in
open-plan schools spent less time talking to each other, but
spent more time than children in ordinary classrooms in taking
an interest in what the teacher was doing and in the work and
the activities of other pupils. The open-plan made no
difference to their progress in basic skills.

Another study in England found that only a third of teachers
in open-plan schools actually like them, and open-plan schools
are more stressful to work in, and that "a quarter of the day
in open-plan infant schools could be spent on such things as
calling the register, moving about from one activity to another,

tidying up, changing for PE or just waiting". Both studies found that there are good and bad designs for open-plan primary schools, and that this depended on the extent to which the general working area could be supervised from the home base.

This is a natural response from teachers, who are paid to supervise what happens in schools, but who are not consulted about their design.

Rejecting school

The most important fact about places for learning in both Britain and the United States is that, in spite of the hopes of their parents, of their local communities and of the public authorities providing them, so many children should reject them. Many years ago the British Department of Education and Science commissioned a report on the education of ordinary children ages 13 to 16. Sir John Newsom, editing the result called *Half Our Future* in 1963, headed it with a little story:

A boy who had just left school was asked by his former headmaster what he thought of the new buildings. 'It could be all marble, sir', he replied, 'but it would still be a bloody school'.

Nothing that has happened in a quarter of a century of education since then has changed any responsible educator's perception of the situation.

Schools are different from any other human environment except one. You are there under compulsion. This is why schools are compared with prisons. There is a dreadful paradox here. In rich countries there is always a proportion of children who reject school, evade it as much as they can, and do their best to disrupt its workings and destroy its premises. School vandalism and school arson as well as endless theft of saleable equipment from schools, present a hideously expensive problem for education authorities. Because their own status and effectiveness is involved, they tend to conceal it, both from themselves and from the citizens.

In poor countries, with an acute lack of buildings, books or equipment, or the money to pay teachers, education is seen as something precious to be striven for at any cost.

When Kenya was struggling for independence from British rule in the 1950s there was a period known as the Mau-Mau Emergency, when the British army rounded up huge numbers of men and boys as 'suspects' and put them in camps surrounded by barbed wire. An army captain found himself in charge of a camp full of teenagers and had to draw upon his own experience of the British education system to think how to occupy their time. So he organised them in houses and classes according to age and appointed his soldiers and the older boys to be teachers of reading, writing and arithmetic. His embarrassment was that his solution worked. Beyond the barbed wire were crowds of parents and children demanding that they too should be given this marvellous privilege. He had turned his prison into a school.

In the rich countries the tendency is to turn city schools into prisons. Vandal-proof schools are designed, without windows or destructive surfaces and furniture, reversing the trends of the last hundred years. Policeman stalk the corridors. It is all in vain. Those who want to can still destroy the school, and far more can find ingenious ways of staying away. Absence from school has a variety of explanations. One is hatred of a subject, or a teacher, or of the whole complex of buildings itself. Another is the need to make money in the usual obvious ways, street trading, begging, prostitution, drug-dealing. Another is looking after the baby while a single parent is out earning. The final one, in an era of mass movements of populations, is that of acting as an interpreter for foreign-born parents in dealings with public officials and social security organisations.

Looking for responses beyond the punitive ones of more policing or of putting more children in prison, there have been attempts to create alternatives to schools. Some dedicated teachers have turned the 'Sin Bin' or truant centre into a place of learning for people who have rejected school. The examples that have actually worked have several characteristics. The first is that they are small and not like school. Maybe they are a club set up in a private house or a lock-up shop. The second is that they are built around the needs of an individual child, not around a school subject transmitting a body of learning. The third is that they depend upon a direct, person-to-person relationship between the teacher and the student. They recreate the ancient and simple situation of skilled people passing on their wisdom to the young. Just as in the Kenya camp from years ago, there are children in ordinary schools who *envy* the treatment given to those who have broken the rules. The lesson is that learning depends on relationships and not on buildings.

The progressive response

In the two decades between the world wars a series of 'progressive' schools in several countries attempted, by experiment, to change the direction of schooling, often rediscovering the principles of the early pioneers. Famous British examples were the Malting House School in Cambridge run by Susan Isaacs, Beacon Hill School run by Dora Russell and Summerhill School run for half a century by A.S. Neill whose propaganda for his approach to education has been read all round the world. None of these used buildings designed as schools. They were not rich enough, and they used whatever buildings they could afford to rent. Dartington Hall, another British progressive school, was wealthy enough to be designed from the start. Its premises were like those of any other school, though in beautiful rural surroundings. It was a boarding school and the aspect that pupils remembered best was that they each actually had a room of their own.

In Germany and Switzerland Rudolf Steiner developed a philosophy called *Anthroposophy* and began the Waldorf School movement which has spread throughout the world. He had elaborate ideas about learning environments, and when his first school was burnt down he redesigned it in reinforced concrete because he believed that the curvilinear possibilities that this kind of construction made possible were appropriate to the needs of children. From the eighteenth-century philosopher Goethe, he developed theories about the place of colour both in the child's surroundings and in the work produced by children in schools.

Many of the progressive educators have affected the *conduct* of primary education, but they had no influence on the *design* of learning places.

Communities of scholars

Higher education has followed a similar path of institutionalisation as schooling. In the universities of the Middle Ages, bands of scholars assembled around particular teachers to learn what they had to offer, and then wandered off to another place of learning. Oxford was started by rebel students from Paris, Cambridge by rebels from Oxford, Harvard by rebels from Cambridge, and so on.

When a tradition of learning was established anywhere, benefactors endowed colleges. It is hard to recognise the origins of modern institutes of scholarship in their humble and haphazard beginnings, but to this day the prestige of higher education is ranked by the age and discomfort of its premises. In both Cambridge, England, and Cambridge, Massachusetts, it is possible to meet distinguished scientists in their new and expensively-equipped departments and laboratories who recall with nostalgia the sheds and converted warehouses in which the really important discoveries which made their institutes famous took place, and who will reminisce with phrases like: 'In those days we were a community of scholars, not just an education factory'.

Schools without walls

In the nineteenth century the novelist Leo Tolstoy decided to start a school in his Russian village, so he toured around schools in Germany, France and Britain. His conclusion was that "Education is an attempt to control what goes on spontaneously in culture: it is culture under restraint".

In the French city of Marseilles he went to every school and talked to children and parents. He found that schools were awful. Prison-like buildings, and children mechanically learning simply the contents of their books without being able to read, spell or add up anything else.

With the insight of a great writer, he reached an important conclusion:

If, by some miracle, a person should see all these establishments without having seen the people on the streets, in their shops, in the cafés, in their home surroundings, what opinion would he form of a nation which was educated in such a manner? He certainly would conclude that that nation was ignorant, rude, hypocritical, full of prejudices and almost wild. But it is enough to enter into relations and to chat with a common man in order to be convinced that the French nation is, on the contrary, almost such as it regards itself to be: intelligent, clever, affable, free from prejudices and really civilised.

How could this possibly happen? Tolstoy found the answer after school, wandering around the city itself, its cafés, museums, workshops, quays and bookstalls. He found that real education came from the environment.

Over a century later, a series of Western educators rediscovered this message. Known as the *Deschoolers*, they included Ivan Illich in Mexico, John Holt, Paul Goodman and Everett Reimer in the United States. They set up 'storefront schools' using vacant shops as teaching places, or they developed 'learning networks' through which people seeking some particular knowledge could acquire it from a practitioner. Or they invented the School Without Walls, using the city itself as the means of teaching children. In the 1960s the Parkway Education Program in Philadelphia set up a home-base with office space for staff and lockers for pupils, and then sent the art students to the art museum, biologists to the zoo, mechanics to a garage and business students aged 14 to 18 to offices and newspapers. In Chicago, in the Metro High School, they were similarly sent by bus and the underground and elevated railways to the places where they could learn from the city itself. Métro Éducation Montréal exploited the city's underground railway to give rapid access to a variety of under-used facilities throughout the city centre: empty cinemas, vacant office space, un-exploited computer centres, parks, restaurants, libraries, clinics and laboratories.

All the resources for learning were there already. But of course these activities contradicted a century of increased specialisation in school design, they demanded a high degree of organisation and stage-management beyond the normal expectations of teachers. The management of education, with its huge public budgets as well as the expectations of parents, could not cope with the experiments in de-schooling.

Community education

Can we, as parents and citizens, make some kind of compromise between the radical ideas of the deschoolers and our own expectations of schooling for our own children? A variety of educational thinkers have seen the school as simply a part of the learning or leisure resources for the whole community. The trend for schools to become larger and more lavishly equipped underlines the absurdity of keeping the school as a separate and segregated ghetto with its expensively provided plant and facilities available for use for only one age group of the population for only part of the day, part of the week and part of the year.

Their view is supported by the experts on vandalism who urge, practically, that school buildings should be kept open as long as possible out of school hours, just so that people should be there continually and just in the hope that the young will see them as their own property instead of as targets for assault and revenge.

This leads to a different concept of the school. It is no longer an isolated building surrounded by playgrounds and fences. It is instead a community facility, set among the shops and public buildings in the centre of a district. There is no school hall: a hall used for every purpose by the public is used by the school when it needs it. There is no dining hall: the children use a café open to the public, and behave accordingly. There is no gymnasium: the school uses the sports hall open to all. There is no school library: the public library has a far greater stock. Among the shops and offices and the district centre are scattered the classrooms and laboratories which are also used by other organisations. The daily lives of the community and its children are inextricably mixed, just as they were for most people all through history.

It goes without saying that the traditional distinctions between the different stages of schooling are equally blurred: day nursery, infant and junior school, middle and secondary school, further education college and adult education centre are, in terms of their physical plant, fellow users of the same environment.

It requires an immense effort to insert a school into the fabric of a community in this way. One example which has succeeded in a bleak climate of public spending is the Abraham Moss Centre in Manchester, England. The difficulties are not matters of design. The whole message of this chapter has been that teaching and learning can happen in any kind of environment. The problems arise because of the compartmentalised structures as well as the different pay scales of the variety of public and private bodies involved.

But the approach that assumes that the school is not a special place, simply a particular user of every public space, is gaining support in several countries. It improves the attitude of children towards the community and it improves the attitude of the community towards its children. It points to the pattern of education in the twenty-first century.

Further reading

Eileen Adams and Colin Ward, *Art and the Built Environment: A Teacher's Handbook* (London, Longman, 1982).

Edward Blishen (editor), *The School That I'd Like* (Penguin, 1969).

John Bremer and Michael von Moschzisker, *The School Without Walls* (New York, Holt Rinehart, 1971).

David Canter (editor), *Psychology and the Built Environment* (London, Architectural Press, 1974).

Kevin Lynch, *Growing Up in Cities: Studies of the Spatial Environment of Adolescence* (Cambridge, Massachusetts, MIT Press, 1978).

Robin C. Moore, *Childhood's Domain: Play and Place in Child Development* (London, Croom Helm, 1986).

Andrew Saint, *Towards a Social Architecture: The Role of School Building in Post-War England* (London, Yale University Press, 1987).

Stuart Sutton, *Learning Through the Built Environment: An Ecological Approach to Child Development* (New York, Irvington Publishers, 1985).

Barbara Tizard et al, *Young Children at School in the Inner City* (London, Lawrence Erlbaum Associates, 1988).

Yi-Fu Tuan, *Topophilia: A Study of Environmental Perception, Attitudes and Values* (New Jersey, Prentice-Hall, 1974).

Colin Ward and Anthony Fyson, *Streetwork: The Exploding School* (London, Routledge & Kegan Paul, 1973).

Colin Ward, *The Child in the City* (New York, Pantheon, 1979; second edition London, Bedford Square Press, 1990).

Colin Ward, *The Child in the Country* (London, Robert Hale, 1988; London, Bedford Square Press, 1990).

8.   Education for Resourcefulness

I am sure that there are people here who remember Anthony Weaver who died last December at the age of 78 after what seem to have been several different lifetimes in education. He wrote to me last summer to tell me that he was retiring for the third time, as a visiting fellow of the University of London Institute of Education where his last concern had been with education for international understanding. Many decades earlier he taught in the London County Council secondary schools, at a Lycée in France, and then for ten years at a progressive school, Burgess Hill. After that he was headteacher at a school for maladjusted children, warden of a residential clinic, was a teacher of teachers at Redlands College, Bristol, senior lecturer in education at Whitelands College and then lecturer in education and art therapy at Goldsmiths' College School of Art.

He was in fact precisely the kind of person attacked by the then Secretary of State for Education in January as members of the "progressive educational establishment" whose influence on the training of teachers was sabotaging the government's educational reforms. Mr Clarke got it wrong of course. People like Tony Weaver had all too little influence however much they managed, simply through a rich harvest of experience, to penetrate the educational establishment. Yet Mr Clarke was in another sense quite right. Tony Weaver and others like him (for other people here will remember Robin

Keynote lecture at the Human Scale Education Movement Conference on 'Education as if People Matter' at Dartington Hall, Devon, 4th April 1992.

Tanner, who rose to the heights of becoming one of Her Majesty's Inspectors) were deeply subversive of the governmental ideology of education. His work for the World Education Fellowship was, after all, conducted from the Centre for Multicultural Education, he was a life-long pacifist propagandist, and, worst of all, he had fallen under the influence of Herbert Read's book *Education Through Art* seeking a schooling constructed around creativity.

Thirty years ago, when I was editing the monthly *Anarchy*, one of a number of articles Tony Weaver wrote for it attacked the notion that the basis of education should be the fact that then, as now, "the welfare of the state in economic competition with other states requires skilled technicians". He wasn't attacking technical education – we are all poorer for our lack of it – he was contrasting our approach to it and our assumptions about what it's for and how it's done.

His article was called 'Jug and Clay, or Flower?' and this quite well-worn analogy is still useful for us, not just in opposing the whole concept of a National Curriculum but in considering our own agenda on 'Education As If People Matter'. Weaver wrote:

The young child's mind may be likened to a jug into which the teacher pours information, as much or as little and of the kind that is thought fit. This ancient conception regards the mind as a vessel which should be made, by force if necessary, to hold what is ordained by tradition to be the best content for it. Similarly the child's character is regarded as some plastic material separate from the faculties of the mind, to be moulded into shape – by the teacher, and by the type of group discipline exerted, according to definite ideas of what is good form. The child is not only moulded into a pattern but comes to feel that conformity is desirable and that divergence from it is idiosyncratic, suspect and subversive ... The analogy of the flower suggests an upbringing that enables a person to blossom in his or her own way. The gardener's job is to provide the most appropriate soil and nourishment that he knows of, and to protect the tender plant from extremes of frost and scorching heat.[1]

Probably we all agree with these analogies. But the most thought-provoking observation I ever learned from Tony Weaver came from his book *They Steal for Love*, based on his four years as warden of a residential clinic to which the London local authority sent children regarded as 'pre-delinquent' and placed 'in care'. His book was built around seventeen case histories, and one of them was James, aged 12 on admission, who, according to the psychiatric report, had an IQ of 88 and was consequently one of the least gifted of the children described. Probably we are less inclined today to put such emphasis on the ability to do well in tests of Intelligence Quotient, and Weaver commented that James was "remarkable for the very full use to which he put his limited intelligence". He added that:

It is also true that a remarkable number of children, who one would think *ought* to be maladjusted, are not. Having apparently the same adverse factors to contend with, on account of some inner resources and unexplained strength, they emerge, as it were, unscathed.[2]

I have pondered over these remarks ever since, wondering how these inner resources can be discovered and built upon, and how others can, like James, be enabled to put to "a very full use" a limited intelligence quotient. It's a real issue that lies behind many of the problems people agonise over, as getting by in life becomes an ever more complicated task. My wife, Harriet Ward, many years ago coined an aphorism to state this dilemma: "As the threshold of competence rises, the pool of inadequacy increases".[3]

Behind this thought lies a huge issue which doesn't only affect James and his IQ scores of forty years ago. It affects us all, even the footloose intelligentsia too superior to acquire computer skills. Moralists used to complain that capitalist industrial production reduced the craftsperson to "a sub-human condition of intellectual irresponsibility".[4] slogging away in heavy industry in the last century or doing some atomised task on the assembly line in this one. Now those jobs have gone, whether in industry or in agriculture or in the office. As traditional sources of employment have disappeared, not just in the disastrous '80s but all through the post-war years, a new set of political prophets has arisen, praising the trimmer, leaner, thrusting economy (notice the metaphors from the boxing ring) and scolding those atavistic Luddites who want to cling to their traditional jobs in the old heavy industries: steel, shipbuilding, heavy engineering, mining and so on.

What they are really saying is, of course, something far less acceptable. The self-made heroes of the Thatcher period are saying 'We owe nothing to inherited wealth. We've battled our way up from the bottom of the social heap. Why can't you?' Beyond this they are saying something else. They are saying 'Okay, you're thick, or you wouldn't be down there. But why can't you make a bit more effort? Why don't you make a fuller use of your limited intelligence?' They too are influenced unconsciously by Michael Young's brilliant book from 1958, *The Rise of the Meritocracy*, about the rise of a new non-self-perpetuating elite consisting of "the five per cent of the population who know what five per cent means". His satire, you will remember, introduced the formula $M = IQ$ plus Effort. If you read the book you will remember that the meritocratic society was challenged by the Populist movement of the year 2009, attacking the aim of equality of opportunity to become unequal, in favour of a society in which all individuals had equal opportunities not to gain access to privilege but to develop their own "special capacities for leading a rich life".[5]

Naturally, just like you, I have thought about these issues for years, which is why I have never been impressed by the education policies of any political party. But the issues they are struggling with from their particular assumptions are real enough, and are at the heart of a whole range of the economic and social problems that form the backdrop to our educational dilemmas. We are in fact talking about resourcefulness, which is an aspect not just of our aims in schooling but of whole cultures of child-rearing and parenthood and our attitudes to childhood.

In search of the secrets of education for resourcefulness, my best guide has been not an educator nor a member of the battalion of sociologist of education but a historian, Paul Thompson. You will know him, if you do, in a number of different guises, most likely as a practitioner and advocate of oral history and family history, or perhaps as a historian of Victorian architecture and design. He wrote the best general book about William Morris, a continually-reprinted Oxford paperback *The Work of William Morris*,[6] which should not be confused with the biography by his namesake E.P. Thompson.

Paul Thompson was the obvious choice by the William Morris Society to give its Kelmscott Lecture in 1990, the centenary of the publication of Morris's utopian novel *News from Nowhere*, and it is now available in print.[7]

It's the kind of publication that an earlier generation would have called 'a little gem', as it is so full of unexpected insights and connections. As you might expect, Thompson traces the links between Morris's vision and today's worries about environmental and ecological issues, about the concept of world citizenship and the transformation of ordinary life.

But the most striking aspect relates to Thompson's own work. He is a pioneer of 'oral history' and in the 1960s conducted life-history interviews with 440 people born between 1870 and 1906. Unexpectedly he found, in his book *The Edwardians*, that there was one community in Britain where child-rearing was more gentle, generous and civilised than in the ordinary British family of those days of any class. This was among the crofter-fishing families of Shetland.[8] Intrigued by this he was able, many years later, to study the fishing industry all around the British coasts in his book *Living the Fishing*.

In the capitalist trawling industry, now dead, he found long hours, low pay, "terrible violence both at work and in the home" resulting eventually in the "destruction of the workforce and the demise of the industry itself". In the Western Isles he found areas "where religious pessimism combined with a rigidly hierarchical family system to repress and stifle new ways of working". In the Shetland Islands, as had been hinted by his interviews with an earlier generation, he found that "the culture deliberately encouraged thinking and adaptability and innovation among ordinary people".

Then he makes the important connection between child-rearing and a creative economy, for he goes on to observe that:

In the Shetlands in particular ... there is a very special way of bringing up children, which instead of emphasising control and physical discipline, encourages reasoning and discussion. Children are brought up from a very early age to be part of adult society. If you go to a Shetland concert, there will be little children wandering around; nobody minds, and the children behave themselves. Shetlanders typically believe in social and moral self-responsibility and expect children to think for themselves from a very early age. They also have a high degree of literacy, and indeed the highest library circulation in Britain. It is my belief that this exceptional family and community culture explains how ordinary working families, who fifty years ago had a standard of living little above an elementary subsistence level, have since the last war shown a striking technical inventiveness and adaptability in taking up new ways of fishing. One of the Shetland fishing islands has, astonishingly, the highest capital investment per household of any community in Britain: yet this is an investment in boats owned by ordinary working families. It is an extraordinary manifestation of the potential of ordinary men and women.

This observation led me back to his 400-page study of the fishing industry. Economic theories of 'modernisation', he notes, contrast societies seen as "slumbering in traditional immobility and poverty", with developed societies "which have earned their present affluence through adaptability, acceptance of the logic of science, the cash nexus and individualism". He used the Shetland example to show that there are other paths to prosperity, "in some cases based on the re-creation of more 'traditional' attitudes, such as work organisation round the family boat rather than wage labour".

Who would have guessed fifty years ago, he asked, that the modern capitalist trawler fleets of ports like Fleetwood, Hull and Aberdeen would reach bankruptcy and closure, while the prosperous crew from a remote island who "by the normal logic of 'progress' ought to have been driven out of business decades ago – could afford to lay up their half-million pound ship for a week, in order to take in the hay harvest on their crofts?" For people here who know about the problems of the fishing industry, I should interpolate the point that it isn't the Shetland fishermen who are greedily plundering the seas by an indiscriminate scooping up of the whole population of a large area. In Cornwall last summer I was talking to David Chapple of the South West Handline Fishermen's Association, who of all innocent parties found themselves victimised by the quota system. The Minister replied to their complaint that any increase in *their* quota would have to be at

the expense of other areas where the local Fish Producers'
Organisations had declined to accept a reduced quota. To
which the Shetland fishermen, at the other extremity of the
British Isles, were a sole exception, replying that *they* would
be willing. This recent fact adds to Thompson's emphasis on
the constellations of beliefs, values and attitudes, which are so
contrasted between one community and another. And his
final point in studying these contrasts is that:

It is not the egalitarianism of the wider society which has stifled creativity
and forced innovators into social isolation, but its demand for the social
conformity and quiescence necessary to maintain inequality. The
importance of the fishing communities is that they show the viability of an
alternative way: for it is only such socially isolated groups which have been
able to sustain up to the present the truer form of egalitarianism which
fosters real social independence and individuality.[9]

But since then his work has led him to further comparisons in
a quite different aspect of the experience of work. He is
involved in an elaborate comparison of working and family
lives in the motor industry, between Coventry and Turin.
Both places have experienced in the last fifteen years the
collapse of the giant factory economy: the very model and
archetype of modern mass-production industry. In his
Kelmscott Lecture he went on to say:

... I found that while the English city in the face of that crisis seemed
depressed and hopeless, the Italian city was unexpectedly optimistic, indeed
booming with new firms, at all social levels from engineering design to metal
workshops and squatters' vegetable market allotments. Again I have been
struck by apparent links between that inventive adaptability and the ways
in which people are brought up in the two cities. In Coventry – perhaps as
a result of more than three generations of factory work in Britain – interviews
brought a picture of a very rigid type of socialisation. In many families,
children were still expected to be seen and not heard, for example at
mealtimes, and indeed some are expected scarcely to talk or discuss at all
with their parents. Parents seemed surprisingly unable to transmit either
their ideas or hopes or their skills to them, and children were often harshly
disciplined. In Turin, by contrast, children were brought up with a much
more open expression of affection, and a rare use of physical punishment,
while discussion at table was absolutely central to family life ... The case of
Turin is not unique: a similar economic development is found even more
strikingly in Emilia-Romagna, where the remarkable contemporary
prosperity of the region is based extensively on co-operatives ... Such a
democratic manufacturing economy has no parallel in this country.

Thompson's findings are based upon a large number of intensive family life-history interviews. My own impressions are more superficial, but support him. It seems like a lifetime ago – it was in fact almost half a century – that I spent three years in Orkney and Shetland, and even then it was evident that families were better off than their equivalents in the North of Scotland mainland or the Western Isles which were very poor communities in those days. As to the small workshop economy of Northern Italy, I went to explore it in 1988, and there's a chapter in my book *Welcome, Thinner City* which tells you what I found, and where I remarked that "the economic life of Emilia-Romagna – where more than a third of the workforce is self-employed and where *per capita* incomes are the highest in Italy – is based on an accumulation of assumptions about capital and labour, and about the skill and autonomy of the individual worker that are scarcely grasped in our patronising British attitudes towards the needs of small business. It is certainly impressive to see how so many people live in a world which is precisely that of pre-industrial society and is predicted as the likely pattern of post-industrial work: a 'belt and braces' combination of several sources of employment for the same individual, built around resourcefulness and adaptability and upon the needs of the season."[10]

These people don't follow the rules taught in British and American business schools. Just as Thompson noted that a Shetland family laid up their half-million-pound ship for a week to get in the hay, so I found in a six-man workshop with hundreds of thousands of pounds worth of machinery at Trebbo di Reno, that two workers had taken time off to bring in the maize harvest.

Now you may have some misgivings about the good news I have been retailing. Why do I give such emphasis to the incomes and capital accumulation of the crofter-fisherfolk of Shetland or the small workshop economy of Northern Italy? Aren't there other dimensions to resourcefulness? Yes, of course there are. But my point is different. With the collapse of faith in other versions of socialism, alternatives to capitalist managerialism become increasingly attractive. And as

Thompson remarks and the recent history of Eastern Europe
shows, "the suffocating impact and environmental
insensitivity of the undemocratic centrally-planned
'command economy' has never been clearer". My sympathies
are with all these people at the bottom of the pile in the
dominant economy, pushed by government policy and the
logic of the multi-national market economy into a so-called
underclass of claimants, and denied by our culture of any
opportunity of climbing out.

You may have another misgiving. Aren't I peddling the same
kind of approach as half a dozen arrogant and ignorant
Secretaries of State in the years since 1979, and urging that
the schools should become nurseries of market
entrepreneurialism? My first answer is 'No, I'm not', but my
second answer is that we deceive ourselves if we attribute this
attitude to schooling to Mrs Thatcher and her government.
The last time I had the pleasure of talking in this ancient hall
I said: "I do not believe that the roots of, or the cure for, our
chronic economic malaise are to be found in the education
system and, if it is true that the young do not like industrial
jobs, at either a shopfloor or a graduate level (and it is
symptomatic of the superficial nature of the debate that it fails
to distinguish between the two), I think it ironical that instead
of wanting to change the nature of industrial work, of wanting
to make it an adventure instead of a penance, we should want
to change the nature of the young".[11] I was talking, here, on
22nd April 1977 and I was criticising the remarks of the then
Welsh Secretary, Mr John Morris, who six months earlier
announced that he had given "clear uncompromising
guidance ... circulated to every head teacher in the
Principality, that the priority must be tilted towards the
engineer, the scientist and the mathematician. And in addition
our children must be taught the languages of Europe to such
a degree of proficiency that they can sell and service our
products in the countries of our trading partners". Direct
ministerial intervention in school did not begin in 1979.

Politicians have a romantically Victorian approach to
industry. They haven't noticed that the performing arts
provide more employment in Britain and earn far more foreign

currency for the British economy than the motor industry. Some of us think they are also less lethal and more enjoyable. Perhaps Tony Weaver was right, and not unrealistic in his espousal of a curriculum built around the arts. Think of the huge contribution of the art schools, at least until they were reformed in pursuit of 'academic rigour', to many fields outside the visual arts, like music and drama. Perhaps education for resourcefulness *really* would be an education through art, making us all remarkable for the very full use we make of our limited intelligence?

I should also add that the small business owner is not at all like the entrepreneurial hero-figure of Thatcherite fantasy, apart from sharing the privilege of winding up in bankruptcy. The only sociological study of *The Real World of the Small Business Owner* reveals that they don't have ambitions to expand and become captains of industry, for "that would imply employing people and losing the personal relationships they like to have with a small number of workers". In fact the report by Richard Scase and Robert Goffee finds that "many small businessmen are closer to a kind of dropout. They disliked the whole modern capitalistic ethic, and especially being employed by others; instead they preferred to feel the satisfaction of providing a 'service' and doing a 'good job'."[12]

Now the one thing that stands out from Paul Thompson's life-history interviews with crofter-fishing families and with industrial workers is the stress he places not on formal education but on child rearing. In Shetland, he said, "children are brought up from a very early age to be part of adult society", and in Turin "discussion at table was absolutely central to family life". What about the education system? I wouldn't dare comment on the quality of schooling in Shetland, not being into league tables. What would be our standard of comparison? But I do know a few Italian teachers, and they are bitterly critical of their system, envying the British Primary School as propagated twenty years ago in the series of pamphlets that you probably remember, sponsored by the Schools Council and the Ford Foundation, and published by Macmillan, and now forgotten.

Now you and I realise all too well that schooling, in spite of the time it occupies, is only part of the whole process of cultural transmission, and often a very small part: just one of many influences. When I was involved in environmental education, we used to claim that this was not a 'subject' but an aspect of every subject on the timetable, 'from RE to PE' as teachers used to claim. I am sure this is similarly true of education for resourcefulness. It happens, or doesn't happen, right across the curriculum. The oral history movement that Thompson draws upon brings out from plenty of people's memories teachers who evoked fear and resentment, but it also records the influence of some particular teacher who in their testimony from years later seemed to set them in motion like a giroscope. The resourcefulness of that teacher liberated their own resourcefulness, including those who were able to put to "a very full use" a limited intelligence. I would suggest that this particular magic might occupy your group discussions!

Notes

1. Anthony Weaver, 'Jug, Clay or Flower?' in *Anarchy 21* (vol 2, no 11) November 1962.

2. Anthony Weaver, *They Steal for Love* (London, Max Parrish, 1959).

3. See Colin Ward, *The Child in the City* (London, Architectural Press, 1978; Bedford Square Press, 1990).

4. Eric Gill picked up the phrase from Ananda Coomeraswamy.

5. Michael Young, *The Rise of the Meritocracy* (Penguin Books, 1958).

6. Paul Thompson, *The Work of William Morris* (Oxford University Press, 1967, 1990).

7. Paul Thompson, *Why William Morris Matters Today: Human Creativity and the Future World Environment* (London, William Morris Society, 1991).

8. Paul Thompson, *The Edwardians* (London, Weidenfeld & Nicolson, 1975).

9. Paul Thompson, with Tony Wailey and Trevor Lumis, *Living the Fishing* (London, Routledge & Kegan Paul, 1983).

10. Colin Ward, *Welcome Thinner City: Urban Survival in the 1990s* (London, Bedford Square Press, 1989).

11. Colin Ward, 'Towards a Poor School', lecture to the Dartington Society Conference, 22nd April 1977, reprinted in Mark Braham (editor) *Aspects of Education* (Chichester, John Wiley, 1982).

12. Richard Scase and Robert Goffee, *The Real World of the Small Business Owner* (London, Croom Helm, 1980).

9. *Growing Up in Meaner Cities*

My field of concern is not childhood as such. My books tend to be about unofficial or popular uses of the environment. I write about the link between people and their houses, and on such themes as allotments, shanty-towns and holiday camps. Inevitably this makes me a writer about the uses that children make of their environment. In the early 1970s I wrote, with Anthony Fyson, a book called *Streetwork: The Exploding School*, addressed to teachers. At that time, when the climate of primary and secondary education was much less constrained and far more optimistic than it is today, we were exploring the potentialities and the methods for the use of the urban environment as a resource for schools. Those were the expansive days when in several North American cities projects like the Parkway Program in Philadelphia, Metro High School in Chicago and Métro Éducation Montréal, with the support of their local education authorities, sought to use the facilities that the city itself provided, rather than a school building, as the physical equipment for secondary education.[1]

At the same time I edited a book on *Vandalism*, an uneasy marriage of the sociological and architectural approaches towards the attrition of the environment. Its conclusion, in the early 1970s, was bleak, for what I wrote was:

Our conventional and all too plausible picture of the immediate future is

Lecture at the Birmingham Child Care Conference on *The Child in the City*, International Conference Centre, Birmingham, October 1992. A revised version is published in Berry Mayall, *Children's Childhoods: Observed and Experienced* (London: The Falmer Press, 1994).

that it will be like today only more so: a mobile urban mass society, heavily dependent on the motor car in whose interests huge areas of the inner city are cut up by motorways with acres of sterilised no-man's-land, taken up by traffic intersections, crossed by rat-runs for the remaining pedestrians. The affluent meritocracy commutes to the business district or lives in the expensively renovated inner suburbs, the skilled and semi-skilled workers employed by international companies live in vast estates on the outskirts or in the tower blocks left over from the 1960s, while the permanently unemployed and the fringe of drop-outs for whom idleness is less degrading than work, inhabit the transitional districts of run-down municipal or privately-rented housing. Can we seriously imagine that such an environment will be less prone to vandalism than the one we inhabit today? Or that some combination of education, exhortation and more efficient policing will reduce its extent? What is more likely is that the litter-strewn, windswept public spaces of the future metropolis will be more unkempt, battered and bedraggled because of the high cost and low prestige of maintenance work (in spite of unemployment) and that the spin-off of consumer technology will provide facilities for more sophisticated forms of vandalism.[2]

Even in formulating this kind of sober warning, what I had failed to anticipate was that in the next decade, instead of watching public policies which alleviated the degraded surroundings of urban childhood and adolescence, we were to witness a whole series of decisions by central government that seemed calculated to make matters worse, not least by obliging local authorities to curtail their support for a variety of local and voluntary ventures intended to make towns and cities accessible to their young inhabitants. But as a result of that book the same publisher asked me to write another, about the relationship between children and their environment, asking whether something had been lost in that relationship, and speculating about the ways in which the link between city and child could become more fruitful and enjoyable for both the child *and* the city.

I saw the book that resulted as an attempt to convey the intensity, variety and ingenuity of the experience of urban childhood: a celebration of resourcefulness. In this I was greatly helped in the early editions by a large collection of photographs, mostly by Ann Golzen. And indeed, the original version of *The Child in the City* had one chapter consisting entirely of pictures, and called 'Colonising Small Spaces'. For I am essentially a watcher of what geographers call land-use conflicts, and it is important for me to observe the way that children gain a transient claim to urban space.[3]

My exploration of the interaction between children and the built environment was gratifyingly well-received, and of course I got recruited to discuss it at conferences of teachers and social workers. There I found that the book was seen as one more catalogue of urban deprivations. And indeed, I often met people who assumed that it was the city, the 'concrete jungle' as they frequently called it, that was responsible for the curtailment of childhood experience, but that I ignored the hidden deprivations of the assumed opposite, rural life. So I was obliged to undertake yet another book, trying to get beyond the sentimental mythology that surrounds our approach to the experience of childhood in the country.[4] My own view is that in the era of mass communications differences of family income are more significant than differences in location and that, as Ray Pahl puts it, "in a sociological context the terms rural and urban are more remarkable for their ability to confuse than for their power to illuminate".[5]

Our geographical generalisations may cause other confusions. When we speak of the 'inner city child' we take it for granted that we are talking of poor children, but most inner city children are not poor and most poor children do not live in the inner cities. And if we attempt a qualitative evaluation of the condition of childhood over the whole of the twentieth century, we are faced with the "increasingly important division" that a team of oral historians found in childhood today. They observe that:

For the children of the poor and unemployed who live in the city slums, childhood often remains short and brutal. Some of the poorest children on 'sink' estates become 'street wise' at a very early age. Addiction to hard drugs like heroin and street crime are now beginning to be recognised as problems among younger and younger children. Being found guilty of mugging is not uncommon now among eight or nine year olds in the most deprived areas of large cities, like Brixton and parts of Notting Hill in London. But for the majority, childhood in the late 1980s is a lengthy period of protection and indulgence. A host of institutions, from playgrounds to toy hypermarkets, exist to satisfy the needs and wants of today's child. Most children of the 1980s enjoy rights and privileges which would have been undreamt of at the beginning of the century.[6]

We took it for granted for decades that public policy would extend the protection and indulgence granted to childhood so that it reached that deprived minority, but there is evidence that the situation of the poor child in terms of housing, access to nursery education and likelihood of future employment (and consequently, attitude towards secondary education) has significantly worsened between the 1970s and 1990s. This worsening has been measured in several respects in an investigation from the United Nations Children's Fund. It examined statistics on infant survival, health, nutrition, pre-school care, family planning and other factors affecting childhood, and found that the condition of children in English-speaking countries had worsened in the previous ten years, with one in ten children in Britain living in poverty and one in five in the United States; this "when in western Europe the conditions of children has consistently improved". Most of us believe that the proportions are far greater than UNICEF believed.

Findings of this kind are significant to researchers who may be concerned with quite different and less measurable aspects of later childhood experience. For me the three Rs of children's use of their environment are resourcefulness, responsibility and reciprocity. The absence of universal pre-school care, whether in the form of playgroups and nursery education or a progression from one to the other, implies that those children who need this experience most arrive at the primary school by compulsion with a woeful lack of experience in establishing relationships with other children. The reciprocal factor is missing, so that they fall into the pattern of becoming bullies or victims or isolates. Similarly responsibility for others as well as for our own behaviour is learned through interaction with others, whether they are our own age-mates, older or younger children, or the adult world.

But the most teasing and tantalising of these characteristics that most of us would like to see in children is that of resourcefulness in making use of their environment, simply because it involves those other attributes of responsibility and reciprocity. Every city was once rich in both incidental and intentional resources for children, but our problem is that some children exploit them and others do not. Forty years ago a geographer, James Wreford Watson, plotted on the map of a Canadian city the facilities and cultural organisations available to citizens and compared them with a map registering the concentration of case loads of the Department of Relief, the Unemployment Bureau and the Juvenile Court, and confirmed that a "social Himalaya" prevented the city's poor inhabitants from making use of the facilities taken for granted by middle-class residents next door.[7] And twenty years ago Ashley Bramall, leader of the then Inner London Education Authority, confided to me that whatever new facility was provided for children, he and his committee knew in advance which children would utilise it.

A researcher into leisure made the same point in a different way:

In my leisure research, more of the children who took part in sports than non-sporty children said they lived near open country, to parks and to swimming pools. But what their answers meant was not that the nearer you get to facilities the more you like sport, but that the two groups perceived the world differently and those who used facilities knew where those facilities were: the facilities were part of their universe.[8]

Those children whose universe does contain an understanding of the topography of the local environment, the manipulation of the facilities it offers and the social assurance to use them, need increasingly as the century ends the money to pay for them. Sporting facilities which were once available free or at a nominal entrance charge as part of the community services provided by local authorities or voluntary bodies, are increasingly becoming more elaborate, more centralised and more expensive. For example, there was an assumption in the 1930s and 1940s that councils should provide cheap and simple 'lidos' or open-air swimming pools, and that it was society's duty to ensure that every child should have a chance to learn to swim. By the 1990s they have mostly been closed and replaced by high-quality 'leisure centres' incorporating pools of a far better standard of comfort and luxury, but further from home and at a price for admission that the children who most need them cannot readily pay.

It is not surprising that the division between users and

non-users has become more obvious, nor that some feel automatically excluded, while others, in both acceptable and unacceptable ways, seek the purchasing power to utilise the goods and services that every urban centre provides, at a price.

The child as customer has a regard from the adult world quite different from that given to the child as beneficiary or supplicant, and this lesson is not lost on children. It is part of everyone's experience that those most gratifying occasions in childhood were those when we were not treated as children but met the adult world on equal terms. Some activity in, say, sport or music, was recognised as worthy of uncondescending respect without regard to age, and the children's self-esteem blossomed. In everyday life this accolade is most often given to the child with a job, as important for the feeling of responsibility involved as for the independent earnings that ensue.

This is a topic that is hard to discuss, since our predecessors had to campaign against the exploitation of children, since trade unionists have to claim that child labour is used as a cheap substitute for that of adults, and since teachers are accustomed to complain that the reason why some child falls asleep in class is not through watching night-time television but through the early morning paper round or cleaning job. But children themselves tell a different story, which is one of pride in the responsibilities accorded to them and their feelings of satisfaction in a task accomplished and their right to the income it brings. The issue has, of course, to be seen in a world context. Peter Lee-Wright conducted a television examination of the way in which the rich world's consumers are dependent on the labour of sixty million child workers. He later wrote a book with detailed accounts of his interviews in several continents. One interview encapsulates both the admiration we feel for the resourcefulness of child workers and our fears for their safety. This was at the Ataturk Sanayi Siksi workshop in Istambul where:

Ahmet, 13, and Emit, 14, are normally working late, cutting and arc-welding fuel tanks from quarter-inch steel plate. These small boys handle the heavy metal and the lethal power of the welding torch with insouciant ease. The earthing wire is casually dropped on to the base plate as the intense blue flame fuses the panels together. Just weeks before, their boss had kicked the wire away and was still in hospital with the burns received from the resulting near-fatal shock. The boys did not anticipate making the same mistake, and professed to be happy with their work, despite a 55-hour week for which they made 20,000 Turkish lira (£6.50) each. Certainly in their case the pride of a craft well done and a considerable amount of self-determination made them appear fulfilled in their work. Both expressed the wish to own a workshop of their own in due course, and Emit surprised us by saying how sorry he felt for African children who starved 'and were not lucky enough to work like us'. Not so many working children have such realistic ambitions or such global awareness. But if they were unlucky enough to have the same accident befall them as their boss, they would not be entitled to treatment since they cannot legally be registered.[9]

The story, and the manner of its telling, illustrate our mixed feelings about the economic lives of children. We are likely to conclude that our ethical objection to their undertaking both the kind of work and the hours described is that those boys had been 'deprived of their childhood'. By this we mean not only that play as an end in itself is the proper business of children, that between the ages of five and sixteen the child should be occupied in institutionalised education between prescribed hours. We feel that these are years properly devoted to exploring our own potentialities, our relationships with others in the great art of living together, our physical environment and, above all, our own enlarging autonomy and independence.

These various definitions of the criteria we use to shape our attitude to child labour apply with equal force to another measure of the extent to which children are 'deprived of their childhood'. This concerns the age at which children are granted freedom of movement to travel and use public facilities unaccompanied by adults. Somehow this topic arouses less adult emotion than the idea of children being gainfully employed. A recent study unearthed the history of a forgotten group of children from the nineteenth century: Italian street musicians in Paris, London and New York. They came from poverty-stricken mountain villages, specialising in the manufacture of hurdy-gurdies, barrel organs, fiddles and harps, whose children were sent off to the world's cities, walking, except for sea crossings, often taking monkeys and white mice with them, and sending back the postal orders that kept the family alive back home. Moral crusades were mounted in the host cities and this trade in children was brought to an end, although "opponents showed no concern for Italian child glass workers and sulphur miners subject to far worse conditions".[10] The modern reader, with contemporary perceptions of the capacities of children, finds it hard to imagine how these children survived at all, even though we read every day reports of campaigns in Latin American cities to murder street children because their presence is an embarrassment to trade and to the tourist industry.

But children in families with a secure income once had the freedom of the street in ways we find inconceivable today. I found in several countries, while addressing teachers and students on the urban environment as a learning experience, that they would dig into their bags and briefcases and produce a reprint or translation of an article by Albert Eide Parr about 'The Happy Habitat'. Dr Parr was the former director of the American Museum of Natural History, who in his retirement became a campaigner for a more diversified and interesting street scene than the one we know, which is a commercial townscape redeveloped for the benefit of the out-of-town, male, middle-aged and middle-class motorist. He died in his nineties in 1991. The passage that we all remembered was his account of the environmental diversity of a small Norwegian port, Stavanger, in his childhood:

Not as a chore, but as an eagerly desired pleasure, I was often entrusted with the task of buying fish and bringing it home alone. This involved the following: walking to the station in five to ten minutes; buying a ticket; watching train with coal-burning steam locomotive pull in; boarding train; riding across long bridge over shallows separating small-boat harbour (on the right) from ship's harbour (on the left), including small naval base with torpedo boats; continuing through a tunnel; leaving train at terminal, sometimes dawdling to look at railroad equipment; walking by and sometimes entering fisheries museum; passing central town park where military band played during midday break; strolling by central shopping and business district, or, alternatively, passing fire station with horses at ease under suspended harnesses, ready to go, and continuing past centuries-old town hall and other ancient buildings; exploration of fish market and fishing fleet; selection of fish; haggling about price; purchase and return home.[11]

The important thing about his story is that Parr was four years old at the time. We all seized upon this tale as anecdotal evidence of the fact that the deformation of cities and towns to meet the demands of the motorist has *stolen* childhood experience from every subsequent generation of children. The most recent reproduction I have seen of Parr's recollection was in a journal that reprinted it without comment juxtaposed with a quotation from a book of rhyming survival tips for the '90s child: "Never play with footballs in the middle of the street / Don't take anything from strangers – money, games or sweets".[12] The item was headed 'Progress of Enclosure', linking the historic private sequestration of common ground with the situation of the contemporary child with considerably less unaccompanied access to public space in today's environment than was taken for granted by earlier generations.

This deferment of independent access to anywhere outside the home can be studied in conversations with different generations of any family. Ask a grandparent, a parent or a child the age at which they were first allowed to play in the street, to go on an errand, or to the local park, or ride their bicycles unaccompanied, and the age of independence gets higher in every generation. An attempt was made to evaluate this in 1971, with a comparison in 1990 in five areas of England, replicated by a study in West German schools. The researcher, Mayer Hillman, explained the work in terms of the idea that 'universal' car ownership was a guarantee of personal mobility:

In a statement about the role of the car in today's society, travel was described by Paul Channon, a former Transport Secretary, as 'a barometer of personal independence'. Measured by this barometer, there has been a marked improvement in personal independence over the last two decades for those adults who have acquired cars. What happens if *children's* personal independence is measured on this barometer? The study ... approached this issue through the medium of perceptions of safety as reflected in parental regulation of their children's freedom to get around on their own, and the resulting effect both on children's and parent's patterns of activity. The research was given a temporal dimension by focusing on changes during the two decades in the six 'licences' given to children by their parents – to cross roads, use buses, go to school and other places on their own, to cycle on the public highway, and to go out after dark.[13]

The conclusions that these surveys reported were that nine-and-a-half year olds in 1990 had typically the same freedom of movement that seven year olds did in 1971. And the authors of the survey report noted that this change had happened "largely ... unremarked and unresisted" and that "children have lost out ... without society apparently noticing".[14] Their findings were that:

Whereas nearly three-quarters of the children in 1971 were allowed to cross roads on their own, by 1990 the proportion had fallen to a half. There was an even more marked decline in the proportion allowed to use buses on their own: half were allowed to do so in 1971 in contrast to only one in seven in 1990. In comparing the proportion of children allowed to cycle on the roads it should be noted that whereas two-thirds owned a bicycle in 1971, ownership had increased to nine in ten by 1990. However, two-thirds of the cycle owners in 1971 said that they were allowed to use them on the roads: by 1990 this proportion had fallen to only a quarter. Perhaps, most disturbingly, very few children are allowed out after dark by their parents – effectively a curfew for them. Younger children are most affected, with the difference, as one would expect, declining with age: few eleven or twelve year olds now or indeed then would accept such restrictions on their independence. Although more journeys are made for social and recreational purposes than for school, only about half of the seven to ten year olds who were allowed to go to these places on their own in 1971 were allowed to do so in 1990. And no parents of the seven year olds allow their children to go out alone after dark, a restriction that is removed only for six per cent of the eleven year olds.

It was found that the comparable German children had much greater freedom and that the gender distinctions that in England allowed far more independence to boys than to girls, were far less evident in Germany, apart from that of being allowed out after dark. Parents in England tended to give the unreliability of their children or the fear of their being assaulted or molested by an adult as the reason for restriction of their independent mobility, but traffic dangers were more frequently cited by the German parents. Some kind of balance has to be struck. But does it lie in yet more restriction of children's freedom of movement or in 'taming' traffic? Mayer Hillman tentatively asks a key question, which is whether "the damaging outcomes of the growing parental restrictions on children revealed in our surveys may be associated with some of the anti-social behaviour observed among the current generation of teenagers?"

Earlier investigators of the experience of childhood, John and Elizabeth Newson, found that they got an instant response to the very simple question 'Would you call him/her an indoor or an outdoor child?' Mothers responded with answers that revealed both class and sex differences.[15] Today it is almost taken for granted that to have an outdoor child means endless worry and trouble. The outdoor child is up to no good. The indoor child takes advantage of the same home-centred lifestyle enjoyed by adults: central heating, television with an infinite choice of channels or videos, computers and computer games. Our assumption of course is that the child has access to all these alternatives to traditional experiences in a wider environment, or will find them in the homes of more affluent friends.

But if we are attempting to evaluate the opportunities for childhoods in late twentieth-century Britain we are bound to conclude that something precious has been lost in the range of environmental experiences open to children. The press reported the case of a fourteen year old with 38 convictions for burglary who had absconded for the 36th time from a children's home. He was nicknamed Rat Boy because he had developed the habit, like an urban jungle child, of making a lair for himself in the heating ducts of high buildings. Somehow adult choices have created a world in which we only trust the indoor child, safely at home with all that consumer software. The outdoor child is automatically suspect, often for very good reason. Is that the children's fault or ours?

Notes

1. Colin Ward and Anthony Fyson, *Streetwork: The Exploding School* (London, Routledge & Kegan Paul, 1973).

2. Colin Ward, 'The Future of Vandalism' in C. Ward (editor) *Vandalism* (London, Architectural Press, 1973).

3. Colin Ward, *The Child in the City* (London, Architectural Press, 1978; Penguin Books, 1979; Bedford Square Press, 1990).

4. Colin Ward, *The Child in the Country* (London, Robert Hale, 1988; Bedford Square Press, 1990).

5. R.E. Pahl, *Readings in Urban Sociology* (London, Weidenfeld & Nicolson, 1968).

6. S. Humphries, J. Mack and R. Perks, *A Century of Childhood* (London, Sidgwick & Jackson, 1988).

7. J.W. Watson, 'The Sociological Aspects of Geography' in G. Taylor (editor) *Geography in the Twentieth Century* (London, Methuen, 1951).

8. I. Emmett, 'Masses and Masters: a brief comparison of approaches to the study of work and leisure' in J. Haworth and M.A. Smith (editors) *Work and Leisure* (London, Lepus Books, 1975).

9. Peter Lee-Wright, *Child Slaves* (London, Earthscan, 1990).

10. John E. Zucchi, *The Little Slaves of the Harp* (Montréal, McGill-Queen's University Press, 1992).

11. Albert Eide Parr, 'The Happy Habitat' in *Journal of Aesthetic Education*, July 1972.

12. L. Sumeon and S. Stewart, *The Streetwise Kid: A Keeping Safe Rap* (London, Blackie, 1992).

13. Mayer Hillman (editor), *Children, Transport and the Quality of Life* (London, Policy Studies Institute, 1993).

14. M. Hillman, J. Adams and J. Whitelegg, *One False Move ... a study of children's independent mobility* (London, Policy Studies Institute, 19981).

15. John and Elizabeth Newson, *Seven Years Old in the Home Environment* (London, Allen & Unwin, 1976).

10. Empowerment?

I hope you have observed the invisible quotation marks around my title. I often have to draw attention to George Orwell's fifty-year-old essays on the politics of the English language, epitomised in the appendix to his novel *Nineteen Eighty-Four* and its account of Newspeak and Doublethink. The stampede to embrace the market values of our rulers, seeing everything as a commodity and citizens as consumers has turned government and opposition, industry and education, into exercises in public relations.

There must be people here who remember Molly Dineen's series of BBC2 films on the financial crisis of the London Zoo. One of the directors, using the language of managementspeak, explained the necessity for empowerment of the zoo's workforce. "Once you've given them empowerment", he said, "you've got them in the grinder". There may be teachers here who believe that the endless series of new demands on teachers since 1979 have increased their ability to teach when freed from the government's bogeymen of the dead hand of local authorities or the teachers' unions. I think it is more likely that they will say, as do most teachers I know, that they are obliged to spend their evenings slaving over form-filling instead of recharging their creative batteries for another day. My own teaching days happened in a different atmosphere, when it was inconceivable that Her Majesty's Chief Inspector of Schools would declare that we need "less learning by doing and more teaching by telling".[1]

However, a week earlier, in his lecture at the Royal Society of Arts, the Chief Inspector made a most interesting remark.

Lecture at the Art and the Built Environment Conference on Contemporary Concerns and Future Development, Bretton Hall University College, Wakefield, Yorkshire, May 1995.

He said:

But the problem is not merely a resistance to change. It is, as I say, a commitment to particular beliefs about the purposes and conduct of education; beliefs which constitute the real impediment to the development of a better educational system and which lie, of course, far beyond the legislative ambitions of even the most interventionist of governments.[2]

He and I would differ as to the impediments to a better educational system but we are agreed that teachers, far from being wage-slaves of the schooling machine, actually dare to have a commitment to particular beliefs about the purposes and content of education. And perhaps his remarks about the legislative ambitions of the most interventionist of governments were in fact a coded message to ministers to leave teachers alone for a while.

For you will know as much as I do and he does, that since 1979 there has been the most interventionist of governments and a long parade of Secretaries of State, from Keith Joseph to John Patten, a continuous denigration of teachers, coupled with the imposition of testing at various fixed ages (as though children were not tested enough already) and the final totalitarian imposition of a National Curriculum, in spite of the fact that we already had a depressing uniformity in the subjects that are taught everywhere anyway. Even Prime Ministers have taken time off from their heavy responsibilities to influence the National Curriculum, with Mrs Thatcher decreeing a revival of 'national' history teaching, and Mr Major demanding compulsory team games (at a time when many local education authorities had sold off playing fields, seen as superfluous, in order to boost their education budgets in the era of 'empowerment').

Personally, I rejoice in the fact that, regardless of government, plenty of teachers have a commitment to particular beliefs about the purposes and conduct of education. I don't know what else they should have a commitment to, apart from thankfully drawing their pay at the end of the month. And I rejoice that in our own field, initiatives that emerged in a more expansive schooling climate are alive and well, and developing. One of the survivors of the First World War generation, after the bloodbath engineered by politicians, wrote a book with the title *Look, we have come through!*

Maybe that is the title I should have chosen today, since there are so many people here who are survivors of a more expansive era of educational experimentation, but are still at it, regardless of discouragement. Look, we have come through! To me this is confirmation of the importance of that "commitment to particular beliefs about the purposes and conduct of education" that so frustrates the Chief Inspector of Schools. Asking me to come to this conference, Eileen Adams reminded me that "It is now 21 years since the Front Door project at Pimlico School initiated through the Design in General Education project at the Royal College of Art. This was followed by the Art and the Built Environment funded by the Schools Council from 1976 to '82." It's an irresistible day for me to meet again here the people behind these initiatives and of parallel commitments like those of Jeff Bishop, who was my mentor in the field we called environmental psychology in those days, and Joan Kean of Newcastle Architectural Workshop, promoting the same aims, as well as Bill Lucas of Learning Through Landscapes, a project which has created its own niche in the far more arid climate of the 1980s and 1990s.

In every individual's life the school years are one particular episode, and by now we have a whole generation whose life of compulsory school attendance has been spent entirely in the years of educational constriction and, far worse, the years when school ceased to be the passport to a job. I don't think that the people who are so willing to tell teachers how to teach have any idea of the effect on the young of the fact that few of them can expect that their school achievements guarantee employment.

The 'flexible labour market' is another of those hateful euphemisms, like 'empowerment', which implies that we are all to be slaves of the most casual job in the most casual market, all those things we used to advise the early leavers against. Paradoxically, this gives a greater importance to those subjects on the school curriculum which are concerned with individual children's personal responses to the world around them. When I was an educational failure, the motivation for learning was the prospect of a secure job with prospects, and I used to be told that I would only be fitted for a dead-end job with no future. Today it is a matter of pride for both government and employers that they have achieved the flexible labour market of dead-end jobs for all, with only half the labour force in full-time jobs.

A week before Chief Inspector Woodhead complained in his lecture at the Royal Society of Arts that teachers were wedded to the "woolly and simplistic '60s ideology of child-centred education" and to faith in "discovery learning" in place of formal instruction, with teachers as "facilitators" rather than that of moral and intellectual authorities. I was reading the opinions of Fiona Colquhoun, who is described as "human resources director at Cable and Wireless". She was telling us that the future of work "will test human beings' flexibility and working relationships more than ever before. It will demand that people are self-reliant, resourceful and prepared to change".[3]

Shorn of the rhetoric, these are the very qualities that those old fashioned progressives were seeking, and which the ideal of chalk-and-talk before a cowed class failed to awaken, especially since, thanks to those progressives, it could no longer be reinforced by the fear of physical pain. And in this connection it might be relevant for people like us to draw attention to the fact that the *arts*, meaning the visual, graphic and performance arts, are bigger earners of overseas currency for the British economy than manufacturing industry, the City of London's invisible earnings, or any other source of national income.[4] This isn't the justification that I would seek for the arts in schools, but it is a fact of life which the language of politicians when they talk of education always conceals.

For me it is infinitely important that there actually are teachers with "a commitment to particular beliefs about the purposes and content of education". And since we are in the West Riding of Yorkshire, I want to reiterate the particular beliefs of two well-known Yorkshiremen, both of them knighted by the London establishment and both of whom I knew slightly and listened to often. They were Herbert Read and Alec Clegg.

Alec Clegg was Chief Education Officer for West Yorkshire and was closely involved in the preparation of the Plowden Report of 1967 on *Children and Their Primary Schools*. This humane and sensible document is blamed in the 1990s for the deficiencies of primary schooling and scholars today. One of its recommendations was the establishment of Educational Priority Areas to take the form of 'positive discrimination' for schools in deprived areas of Britain in better staff/student ratios, improved buildings and more money to spend. Clegg ensured that remarkable experiments were undertaken under this banner in his particular patch.[5] He was a member of the committee that produced the subsequent Newsom enquiry into secondary education (*Half Our Future*, HMSO, 1963) and later, on the centenary of the Education Act of 1970, he gave a lecture which I attended on 'The Education of John Robinson'.

Clegg reminded us that the focus of the Newsom report was to examine the problems faced by children of average and below-average ability. Newsom divided them into John Brown, John Jones and, in the least able quarter of any age range, John Robinson. (I should observe that, writing over thirty years ago, he was using male names and pronouns to subsume both sexes, as was still customary then.) I will quote at length Clegg's version of Newsom's detailed survey:

He's the son of an unskilled worker with a large family, living in a poor area. He starts at his secondary school below average in height, weight and measurable intelligence and he's placed in a low stream in the school. He it is who would profit most by a generous use of the school's practical rooms but he is in fact allowed less use of them than either John Brown or John Jones. Though teaching him is one of the hardest jobs, he's often taught by the poorest teachers, and when a teacher is absent it's he who has to make shift. This isn't my invention: all these facts come from a national survey conducted for us when we were on the Newsom Committee. The school isn't concerned about him as it is about those who will bring the renown of examination successes. He dislikes wearing uniform and is seldom a member of the school society or team. He has free dinners, and although Newsom didn't point this out, he often has to queue for his ticket after those who pay have received theirs. He who most needs the spur of success rarely experiences it. He lacks that most powerful of all educational forces, the parental aspiration which does so much for the middle-class child, and he lacks what HMIs described over 100 years ago as 'that recognition which our natures crave and acknowledge with renewed endeavour'.

At this point Alec Clegg had us all nodding with agreement. Yes, we all knew John Robinson. So he added his most devastating comment:

Now may I continue where Newsom left off? He leaves school as soon as he can but is often among the last to land a job, and when he does land one it doesn't carry the distinction of day release or an apprenticeship; and as he's virtually discarded by his school, he avoids the youth club and further education, both of which remind him of it. He knows the misery of unimportance: and no teacher has ever been a John Robinson, no teacher knows the depth of his resentment.[6]

Plenty of teachers, headteachers and plenty of local education authorities took notice of the conclusions of Newsom and of Clegg. They made efforts to draw John Robinson into the community of scholars, and the curriculum development projects sponsored by the Schools Council, another body which has been written out of history although many of the activities it developed for the so-called 'young school leaver' were intended to draw the Robinsons into useful educational experiences.

Today our rulers pretend that John Robinson doesn't exist. He's a statistic that drags down a school's performance in those infamous 'league tables' of the performance of schools, regardless of their situation. But endless social analyses, whether conducted by disillusioned Conservative politicians like Ian Gilmour, by the government's social survey or by the Rowntree Foundation,[7] all indicate that the deprivations in measurable matters like diet, mortality and housing experienced by John Robinson have increased since the 1970s, that his escape into some kind of purchasing power through employment has dwindled and that his revenge on a society that doesn't care about his resentment is very costly to us all. It would have been infinitely cheaper for the public purse to win him for education than to cope with his revenge and lock him up. There isn't any discussion of John Robinson any more, apart from stigmatising him as a member of the newly re-invented 'underclass'.

My second Yorkshireman was an inspiration for art teachers, almost by chance. If you attended the centenary exhibition and conference on Herbert Read in Leeds in 1993, you will remember the impressive range and scope of his interests. By the Second World War, apart from his literary reputation and his anarchist philosophy, he was well-known as the author of *Art and Industry* in 1934, the standard text on industrial design for decades, and of his continually reprinted *Art Now* of 1933 and *Art and Society* in 1937. Last year, David Goodway of Leeds Department of Continuing Education put together a valuable collection of Read's contributions to the anarchist press and in his biographical introduction he tells us of the accidental origins of Read's most celebrated book:

When the British Council was established in 1940, it was decided to 'project' British art overseas during wartime not by sending valuable works by professional artists but to substitute collections of drawings by British children. Read was given the task of selecting the works and visited schools throughout the country. In the year before his death he was to recall it as 'an experience that may be said to have redirected the course of my life'.

Goodway explains that "In particular, it was a working-class girl of five from a Cambridgeshire village who gave him 'something in the nature of an apocalyptic experience' with the drawing she described as 'a snake going round the world and a boat' ... and the result was the magisterial *Education through Art*, published in 1943. As Read was to stress: 'It is not often realised how deeply anarchist in its orientation ... *Education through Art* is and was intended to be. It is of course humiliating to have to confess that its success (and it is by far the most influential book I have written) has been in spite of this fact' ..."[8]

Education through Art was, when first published, heavily-laden with Freudian and Jungian concepts and what one of his biographers, George Woodcock, called "its formidable battery of psychoanalytical, anthropological and pedagogical authorities".[9] Read ruefully admitted that "my book is a difficult one – too difficult for the people it might most benefit".[10]

This judgement was, however, wrong about the reception of his book. A month after it appeared in 1943, when you would think that the British, including teachers, had plenty of other preoccupations, an advertisement was printed in the personal column of the *New Statesman* asking people who had read his

book to attend a meeting in London to discuss the formation
of a Society for Education Through Art. They did, and the
existence of that body and its journal *Athene* brought together
a whole band of pioneers who thought they had been working
in isolation, but now found that they were a movement. Their
art room in their own school was not just an oasis, it was the
local manifestation, not just of a nationwide trend but of a
worldwide tendency. For in 1951 (the year when in the
pre-Letraset era I was doing the lettering in Chinese White on
the jacket of Read's book *Art and the Evolution of Man*[11])
UNESCO in Paris was establishing an International Society
for Education Through Art.

I valued these bodies, not out of love for organisations, but
because in exactly the same way as the much later initiatives
that we were celebrating, like Front Door, Design in General
Education, and Art and the Built Environment, they enabled
teachers to share innovations and experiences. All were levers
of educational change, and they are vehicles for the
empowerment of the child. Herbert Read, in fact, expressed
his educational aims as simply and clearly as did Alec Clegg.
In a lecture fifty years ago he argued that "creative arts of every
kind should be made the basis of our educational system. If,
between the ages of five and fifteen, we could give all our
children a training of the senses through the constructive
shaping of materials ... then we need not fear the fate of those
children in a wholly-mechanised world".[12]

That was fifty years ago. Twenty years ago, when the subversive
influence of the progressives had penetrated primary schools,
a series of 23 little books were published by Macmillan on
British Primary Schools Today. They were sponsored here by
the Schools Council and in the United States by the Ford
Foundation as this was an Anglo-American Primary School
Project. Those little books contrast remarkably with the rewriting
of educational history by our appalling series of Secretaries of
State for Education who claim to be rescuing schools from all
that 'woolly progressivism', for they covered every aspect of
good practice, the pupil's day, the teacher's role, the
assessment of progress and the evaluation of achievement, and
what they described was forty years of struggle to bring the

dreariest of schools up to the standards of the best. The book on Art was written by a well-known London primary head, Henry Pluckrose, who was known to a number of us here, and he wryly observed "that change took place at all was somewhat surprising" and he paid tribute to those teachers, writers and lecturers "who have been responsible for creating a climate of opinion in which these changes could take place".[13]

And in the days when he, just like Herbert Read, was insisting that the skills of manipulating materials were something far more important than a mere "weekly interlude between spelling and mathematics", jumbo-jets of teachers from abroad were flying in to gather inspiration from the British primary school. They don't come nowadays, simply because their schools and ours are too hard-pressed to engage in a fraternal dialogue.

I don't suppose that Read was close enough to the ordinary school system to notice that in his day we actually had a few secondary art schools. This was before the Coldstream-Summerson reforms, demanding 'parity of esteem' and 'academic rigour', cleaned up the art education scene, and made sure that those wayward kids who found a haven in the art school should be kept out. But the art schools really were a refuge. Let me cite the experience of the writer Hanif Kureishi who remembers that "the art schools were the most important post-war British cultural institutions, and some lucky kids escaped into them. Once I ran away from school to spend the day at the local art college ... They liked being there so much that they stayed till midnight".[14]

He makes it sound like the place that was missing in your education, or mine. And it was a determined survivor of the concept of the secondary art school, Ernest Goodman, who was one of the progenitors of the Art and the Built Environment project. He was head teacher of Manchester High School of Art, a famous school overtaken by local changes. But when the local education authority proposed to close it as an anachronism, every big name in the British art world was enlisted to certify that it was a nursery of genius.

I knew nothing of this, but one Saturday morning in the '70s I had accepted an invitation to talk at an art teachers' session at West Dean in Sussex. My acceptance of their invitation was frivolous. I was simply curious about the house itself which had been given to the nation by Edward James, the patron of the surrealists in the 1930s. Unknown to me, my audience included Ernest Goodman, who was chairman of the Schools Council's Art Committee, and Ralph Jeffrey, a member of the Arts Inspectorate. They urged that my employers, the Town and Country Planning Association, should propose an Art and the Built Environment curriculum development project. Their plot worked, and needless to say we found the ideal person to run the project in Eileen Adams, whose Front Door initiatives at Pimlico School were known to me as I had two children at that school.

I have made it sound as though all these events, from Herbert Read's involvement with art in schools onwards, were happy accidents or coincidences. But it would be truer to stress that all through the changes in the political climate of education, there are teachers who will adapt whatever structures are imposed on them, whether changes in the examination system or concepts like the National Curriculum, to their own commitment, as the Chief Inspector put it, "to particular beliefs about the purposes and content of education". The particular belief that I imagine motivates everyone here today was nicely expressed years ago by Ernest Goodman from Manchester when he remarked that:

It should now be clear to all thoughtful educationists that the long domination of English education by cognitive based studies pursued through verbal and numerical modes needs to be reduced, and the educational diet of our young people needs to be more adequately balanced by a far greater concern for their feelings, intuitions and expressive needs. Art can be seen to have the potential to redress the imbalance prevailing since it is deeply and constantly concerned with 'non- linear' response and understanding, with the intuitive 'leap' and with the whole field of visual imagery.[15]

Needless to say, what Ernest said about art is true of all the arts, subverting their way through the landscape of schooling, and that is what brings us all here today to probe contemporary concerns and future developments. We are concerned with the empowerment of another generation.

Notes

1. Chris Woodhead, HM Chief Inspector of Schools, interviewed in *The Times*, 1st February 1995, on *The Annual Report of HM Chief Inspector of Schools, Standards and Quality in Education 1993/1994* (HMSO, 1995).

2. Chris Woodhead, First Annual OFSTED Lecture at the Royal Society of Arts, reported in *The Times Educational Supplement*, 27th January 1995.

3. Fiona Colquhoun, 'People Pressure' in *The Guardian*, 14th January 1995.

4. Diane Coyle, 'Music is a High Note in Britain's Balance of Payments' in *The Independent*, 10th February 1995.

5. See Michael Duane, *The Terrace: An Educational Experiment in a State School* (Freedom Press, 1995).

6. Alec Clegg, Lecture at the Central Hall, Westminster, on the centenary of the Education Act of 1870, printed as 'The Education of John Robinson' in *The Listener*, 13th August 1970.

7. See, just for example, Ian Gilmour *Dancing with Dogma: Britain Under Thatcherism* (Simon & Schuster, 1993); *Social Trends Vol 25* (HMSO, 1995); *Income and Wealth in Britain* (Joseph Rowntree Foundation, 1995).

8. David Goodway, 'Introduction' to Goodway (editor), *Herbert Read: A One-Man Manifesto and other writings* (Freedom Press, 1994).

9. George Woodcock, *Herbert Read: The Stream and the Source* (Faber, 1972).

10. David Goodway, *op cit.*

11. Herbert Read, *Art and the Evolution of Man* (Freedom Press, 1951).

12. Herbert Read, *The Grass Roots of Art* (Lindsay Drummond, 1947).

13. Henry Pluckrose, *Art in the Primary School* (Macmillan, 1973).

14. Hanif Kureishi, 'Boys Like Us' in *Weekend Guardian*, 2nd-3rd November 1991.

15. Ernest Goodman, quoted in Eileen Adams and Colin Ward *Art and the Built Environment: a teacher's approach* (Longman, 1982).

Michael Duane

THE TERRACE
AN EDUCATIONAL EXPERIMENT
IN A STATE SCHOOL

The Newsom Report on secondary education gave the least able pupils the collective name of 'John Robinson'.

John Robinson's only ambition is to leave school. Frustration of this ambition produces behaviour such that his entire age group long for the day when he is allowed to leave. ROSLA, Raising Of (the minimum legal) School Leaving Age (from 15 to 16) in 1972/3 dismayed 15-year-olds of all abilities, and was a focus for heart-searching and experiment among educators.

One experiment was The Terrace, set up by Northcliffe Comprehensive School in the mining town of Conisbrough, South Yorkshire, to provide non-school education for 15-year-olds to whom school had become meaningless. The venture survived for only two years, not because it failed but because its private sponsors decided they could no longer afford it.

Michael Duane had been unusual as a secondary school head in that he took a special interest in the 'John Robinson' pupils, so much so that his methods were alleged to have adverse effects on the education of the rest. His school, Risinghill, was famously closed under him by the local education authority. In the early 1970s he was a Senior Lecturer in a teachers' college, able to visit The Terrace frequently and observe its development. This is the account he wrote at the time.

Colin Ward, who spent a week in Conisbrough in 1973, contributes a foreword in which he describes the educational concerns of the time and reviews developments after twenty years.

ISBN 0 900384 78 6   FREEDOM PRESS   80 pages   £2.50

Press comments on

COLIN WARD'S

TALKING HOUSES

"Many will welcome this latest addition to the prolific Ward literature on housing. As the author himself candidly says, these ten lectures merely reiterate the – to him – simple truths he has been proclaiming for the last 45 years. He confesses that he has nothing new to say and it puzzles him that he is in perpetual demand as a pundit. He can only explain it by people wanting hands-on contact with the human propagators of ideas. Always in the vanguard of fresh examples, he does, indeed, continue to have a unique role to play."
— **Alison Ravetz** in *The Architects' Journal*

"Ward believes that when people cooperate on a small scale and choose, manage and even build for themselves, they get better housing than when governments make choices for them. Decades of official directives and central control have kept us from a great state secret: human beings are, unless culturally disabled, well qualified to meet their essential needs – food, shelter and conviviality."
— **Peter Campbell** in *New Statesman and Society*

"The relevance of the anarchist analysis ought to be self-evident ... This book is a valuable source of practical examples of user control and provides glimpses of a well constructed ideological framework to set them in ... conveyed with absolute clarity."
— **Benjamin Derbyshire** in *RIBA Journal*

"Labour's policy on housing has not yet gone on the offensive in reappropriating the language and spirit of self-help and local control so that people no longer fear that regulation is its knee-jerk solution to all problems. The party could usefully borrow from Ward's exhilarating polemic in support of changing the role of the administration from providers to enablers, of the citizens from recipients to participants."
— **Shaun Spiers** in *Tribune*

FREEDOM PRESS   142 pages   ISBN 0 900384 55 7   £5.00